To Naum;

Thanks for your friendship & wisdom.

GIVE ME TWO MINUTES OF YOUR TIME

Give Me Two Minutes of Your Time

Let's Have a Conversation…

Harry Z. Sky
David J. Trobisch

Quiet Waters Publications
Bolivar, Missouri
2005

For information contact

Quiet Waters Publications,
Bolivar MO 65613-0034
E-mail: QWP@usa.net.

For prices and order information visit:

http://www.quietwaterspub.com

Front cover photo by Robert Diamante
http://www.robertdiamante.com

First printing 1/2005
Second printing 7/2005 (revised, index)

ISBN 1-931475-26-1

Library of Congress Control Number: 2004117262

PREFACE

We wanted to call the first book we would write together, *The Rabbi Who Made Friends with a Lutheran.* It would have captured what we are about.

As a German Lutheran and a trained theologian I belong to a denomination struggling with its past, seeking for forgiveness because of the outrageous anti-Semitic thoughts Martin Luther and many of his followers have expressed or left unchecked for so many centuries.

I met Rabbi Harry Sky first in a professional setting. We both had accepted the challenge to teach a course together at the University of Southern Maine without knowing each other very well. We called it "Who am I? – In search of a new Jewish-Christian identity." Our students were surprised, shocked, and delighted to see us struggle with topics supposed to be divisive, but always finding common ground. At the end of the semester we had become good friends.

Harry Sky invited me to contribute to the book he was working on. When I showed him what I wrote, he laughed and commented, "You have to have humor!"

And so the reader will find, embedded among the vast collection of meditations and short sermons by Rabbi Harry Sky, a few reflections from a Lutheran Christian designed to make you wonder. My contributions are marked with *DJT.*

Dr. David J. Trobisch
Throckmorton-Hayes Professor of New Testament Language and Literature
Bangor Theological Seminary, Portland Campus, Maine

NOTE TO THE READER

In this divided world, bridges are called for. It's time we returned to the lesson of Genesis: All of us, humans are created in the *tzelem*, the image, of God. The image, the lesson that is God. All of us contain the whisper placed in the first human by the Creator. All of us derive a sense of life (living being) from that phrase.

In this collection, we attempted to build universal bridges, first through text and interpretations, secondly in inviting Dr. David Trobisch of Bangor Theological Seminary to write the preface and to contribute some interpretive pieces to our undertaking. We welcome his erudition and friendship.

Thanks to Sam L. B. Elowitch as well, whose editorial help is greatly appreciated.

The world calls for healing words, words of closeness and friendship. We hope we have contributed our bit to satisfy these desires.

Harry Z. Sky, Dr. h.c. mult.
Rabbi Emeritus of Temple Beth El, Portland, Maine
Rabbi-in-Residence at Congregation Etz Chaim, Portland

Eizehu chacham? Ha-sameach be-chelqo

Who is wise? He who is happy with his portion in life
(Mishnah Avot 4:1).

No matter how we try, no matter how careful a mother carrying a fetus may be, no matter how watchful we are, we're faced with the given. A child comes into life bearing signals within itself. It's almost as if it had swallowed prior to its birth its own potential life-story, and it was sent into the world to see what it can do with it. Therefore, to speak of normal behavior, of accepted behavior, of correct behavior, politically or otherwise, seems to be stretching the point. If I am a bearer of my own wisdom, prior to my being able to articulate it, then what can all of these fixes do except detract me from my destined course?

Many of us moderns would like to believe that destiny is an old-fashioned, best-forgotten word. In the battle of nature versus nurture, more people seem to tend toward nurture than to nature. My father, of blessed memory, would say when puzzled by someone's behavior, "This is *sein natur*, your nature. Don't disturb it, but honor, love it, welcome it." Remember the story of the Hunchback of Notre Dame? By all standards, he should be ignored and shunned. We should be horrified by his appearance. He is nothing like the handsome, sophisticated beings we seek to be. Yet, there was someone who went beyond the *façade* that was he and found the soul he carried within himself. It was a loving soul, a caring soul, one that sought to encourage, to enliven, and to reach the point of faith.

So the lesson I want to share with you is, if you seek to find inner peace, a sense of being at ease with this world, don't forever compare yourself to another, but rather say, "Thank God for the gift that is me."

Eli atah ve-odekha Elohai aromumekha

You are my God and I send my thanks to you.
You are my God, and I constantly proclaim it (Isaiah 25:28).

Believing in God in Jewish terms is not an abstract act. It's not a philosophical statement, nor a theological one, but, in the words of Abraham Joshua Heschel, a "moment of true reality." In his many books dealing with the human search for God, Heschel disagreed with the philosophers that he had studied in his younger years. To him, God was as real as any person he might be addressing at any moment. This doesn't mean that he anthropomorphized God; he is saying to us that God is as real as the nose on my face. Therefore, he understood deeply the tradition of the *chasidim* that spoke of meeting God *panim al panim*, face-to-face.

How do we know that we are in God's presence. How do we relate to the force we call God? I am sure there are many who will say, Can we ever completely know God? Can we describe God? Does God have human features, or is God *sui generis*, a category unlike any other? Carl Jung would say that God is a given, that God is one of many archetypes. In fact, when someone asked him, "Do you believe in God?" he answered "I know." According to the latest biography of Jung, neither he nor his family regularly attended church, even though he and his wife were descendants of a long line of clergy.

The Psalmist in the above quote sensed God in a most personal way: *Eli atah*, you are my God, and I am thankful. You are my God, and I'll proclaim it. I'll shout it from the rooftops. Yet, if he had been asked to describe this god, he'd demur. He'd say, as another Psalmist said, "God has no eyes, no ears, no tongue or voice-box. When he speaks to us, it's not with human speech." The Psalmist is trying to say "I can attest to His existence. It's a mystical thing. It's not a rational thing. It can't be proven by scientific means." Yet, the Psalmist and I too know that "you are my God."

Oftentimes, in these my later years, when puzzled, when looking for something that is in front of me yet I can't find it, I say "you are my God" and *viola*, there is the object I was seeking.

Adonai oz le-amo yiten.
Adonai yevarekh et amo ba-shalom.

God gives strength to His people.
God will bless his people with peace (Psalm 29:11).

What is being considered in the verse? What kind of strength is *oz*? Didn't the prophets say, *lo ve-chayil lo ve-khoach, ke im beruchi amar Adonai* (Zechariah 4:6)—Not strength, not power, but spirit is what Adonai seeks? So what is *oz*? What is *koach*? Could it be that *oz* is military might, such as shown by

Goliath? Such power doesn't open the doors leading to the Divine Presence.

On the other hand, *oz* is the strength that comes from faith. Knowing, believing there is an overarching presence always in our horizon. When one is attuned to it, *shalom* (peace, harmony) comes in its wake, for the power, the strength that is suggested by *oz* is assurance, knowing the presence is there. It's the cloud by day, the guiding flame by night, always present, always pervasive, always assuring. Under such circumstances, one can literally touch the gentleness that is *shalom*.

We Jews have always hoped for *shalom*. It's the final word of the ancient Priestly Blessing, *ve-yasem lekha shalom*. "May the circumstance that we define as *shalom* be placed (*yasem*) in a place where you are." We have always strived for it, but we haven't always been people of *shalom* on our journey. We Jews are as human as anyone else, and many times we act in a human manner when we feel threatened. The psychologists tell us that such reactions are as real as those of an embracing nature, of a loving nature.

ha-zorim be-dimah be-rinah yiqtzoru

He who sows with tears will reap with song (Hosea 8:5).

Life provides us with strange moments and strange partners. We seldom choose them; they seem to come our way. What is their origin? Can it be traced?

Many studies have shown that each moment of our lives we sense messages and we send messages far and wide. When we think of someone far away and wish for his or her wellbeing, we release a form of energy that can prove to be a healer or a reliever of pain and stress. When we wish upon a star, the wish emanates a power of its own—newly created power. The wish becomes a fulfilled dream.

No one seems to know the source of such power. The Psalmist said we may sow with sadness yet reap in a joyful, singing way. Transformations are continuous. The creation of healing vibes never ceases. It seems as if our traditional viewpoint, that we humans are the surrogate creators of the earth and those who assure its survival, we too can speak and it will come into being.

Knowing this to be true, accepting the reality of such beliefs, we find ourselves empowered. We hear an additional voice, separate from the other voices that float in our heads, that says to us, "You can. You will. You shall." Such inner faith, if accepted *in toto* with a true sense of belief, can become our own personal creator. This of course stares in the face of those who say that we humans are "eternal sinners." We are not sinners; we are not tainted; we are not condemned. We are people embarked upon a journey that leads us, we hope ultimately, to Adonai, who is the *Ein Sof*, the ultimate end of all existence.

Fear and awe are two sides of the Hebrew verb (*yud-resh-alef*), and both are a form of respect and distinction. When I stand in awe of someone, I am attributing to that Being a special status. He seems to be in possession of an aura unlike all others. He seems to emanate strength and power, though one might miss it when looking at Him directly. The awe I feel in relation to Him is unlike any feeling I have ever experienced. It's indescribable; it isn't recorded anywhere. One can't find an example of the energy He exudes. It's awesome.

Fear is the other side of the coin. When I'm in a state of fear, I sense, I feel, the crumbling of the foundation upon which I stand and exist. In a state of fear and its attendant trepidation I seem to have lost any controls I may have. It's as if all the brakes within me have disintegrated or are disintegrating. I see no recourse; nothing seems to appear on my personal horizon that can pull me away from the fear I feel. Fear can be provoked by a form outside of myself, or by a form I sense in myself, which I projected on a screen separate from me.

In both case, awe and fear, powers greater than any I'm conscious of have stepped in and are directing my life.

Touched By the Spirit

When the LORD first spoke through Hosea, the LORD said to Hosea, "Go, take for yourself a wife of whoredom and have children of whoredom, for the land commits great whoredom by forsaking the LORD" (Hosea 1:2).

We do strange things because God tells us to do them. When God touches our lives, we have no choice. Thank God if you were never touched by the Spirit!   *DJT*

Kakh mishe-nikhnas adar marbim be-simchah

*When the month of Adar arrives, our mind becomes joyful
(Talmud Taanit 29a).*

We of the Jewish faith take nothing for granted. Our tradition teaches us that all of life is connected, all of nature is connected, all humans are connected. Our life's journey is spent in trying to find the connections so that our path is not besotted with unnecessary burdens. In my younger days, when I attended *yeshivot* of deeply committed Jews, the month of *Adar* could easily have been compared to the extreme celebrations of New Orleans at carnival time. *Adar* was our carnival; the Devil was Haman, the savior was Mordecai. Everything had the finger of God in it. Thus, some of us took literally the folksaying, "In your rejoicing, become so confused that you cannot tell the difference between Haman and Mordecai."

Many historians have told us that the holiday of *Purim*, which occurs in the month of *Adar* and is the reason for all of the celebrations, is a folktale; it never happened. All of the figures were figments of our imagination, whether we refer to Achashverosh, Haman, Esther, or Mordecai. Some have gone so far as to say that its a pagan fairytale, it's Marduk versus Ishtar (note the similarity in their names). When I heard that interpretation in my late teens, I asked "So what?" I sensed that deep in the collective unconscious of our people the story that appears in the Book of Esther was no figment of their imagination, but rather an expression of the reality too often experienced by us Jews.

Haman, in the Book of Esther, is considered a descendant of the Amaleq, that cruel people of ancient times who vowed to wipe the Israelites off the face of the earth. I recall, in the 1930s, many of us said that Amaleq's current descendant was Adolf Hitler. We Jews have been blessed with the gift of memory. Some say it's a curse. I say it's a blessing, for Santayana was correct when he said that "Those who forget the lessons of history are doomed to repeat it." How true! You can't avoid it. You can't avoid your personal history, you can only come to terms with it. You can't avoid collective history, you can only learn some lessons from it. If only our political leaders who lived by Lord Acton's statements that "politics is the art of the possible" and von Clausewitz' statement that "war is a continuation of politics by other means," would say to themselves, "It doesn't have to repeat itself." People change. Consciousness changes, and above all, there is always the element of the *nes*, sometimes translated as "miracle," but better as a sign, that this is indeed possible.

*

Our sages were very practical beings. They knew that we humans more often than not are not in control of our emotions. One Sage said that if a person finds that his yearnings have overtaken him, he should go to a strange place, don dark clothing, and let his emotions go; in other words, get it out of his system. But make sure you don't desecrate God's name in public. If you have to play the fool, don't be God's fool. Admit it's your foolishness that is at work. Don't say "God made me do it." It's your choice.

These very rabbis who suggested we go and get it out of our systems also knew that you cannot say to someone, "If only you would control yourself, all would be well" because at times, we are not in control. There is one other thing: They never denigrated an individual for having chosen the dark road. They also realized that if a person becomes aware of his or her shortcomings, and attempts to return to the self that he or she used to be (known as *teshuvah*), then his or her record of misdeeds can become an ally in the return to the proper path. "When you recognize your misdeeds and see them in the boldest colors, you are apt to say, 'There go I, but I don't want to remain there.' "

Throughout the ancient world, we read of four elements that sustain the universe: fire, wind, water, and earth. Those are the four mentioned in the rabbinic literature. If we look at them carefully, we can understand what the rabbis were trying to say about the world in which we humans find ourselves. Fire is the creative process; wind or air is that which ties one corner of the universe to another; water is a symbol for life; and earth is the symbol for the solid ground so necessary for living.

There are many other interesting groups of four mentioned by the rabbis. For instance, they say that the four pillars of the human are fire, dust, spirit, and water. Dust, of course, is a parallel to earth mentioned above; water is water; and fire is fire. Yet the "wind" and the "spirit" are synonymous. In the creation story, we are told that the "wind" of God hovered over or caressed the water, the source of life. It is in keeping with the later scriptural text that says that "the spirit of God was ingested into a living being."

The stress on spirit is a uniquely biblical idea. I doubt if, prior to the scriptures, we could find a comparable text that suggests that it is the spirit of God, ingested into the human, that creates a human being. This sense of interconnectedness between the human and the Creator was a radical notion in the ancient world. The distance between the human and the creator gods was unbridgeable. In many cases, the human was the fodder to be sacrificed to the gods.

Mah yomru ha-goyim

"What will the other nations say (ironic Zionist saying)?"

In our many years of exile, we Jews attempted to establish enclaves wherever we resided. Some of us became complacent, truly hoping and believing that the old problem of "not wanted" or "unwelcome" had been overcome. Periodically, we've had rude awakenings. "What will the *goyim* (the non-Jews) say?" was ingrained in our very marrow. Sometimes with the snap of our oratical finger, the quiet of the moment ruptured and what seemed to be a temporary haven was transformed into an actual gehenna (hell). Stories abound of pogroms, real estate covenants, social and other discrimination making our temporary "Gardens of Eden" into seething cauldrons of hate and accompanying fear.

"How shall we respond" has been the predominant question. In the years of 1932–1945, one of the more strident anti-Jewish periods in our five-thousand-year history, many Jews who were longtime residents of old, established European cities discovered that their sense of security wasn't worth the paper on which it had been recorded and assured. Jewish families that had lived there for five hundred years, well connected in non-Jewish circles, were deported to the East and into eventual gassing and crematoria, or the showers and the ovens of the "Layers." Jews of Warsaw, Krakow, and other established cities of Poland were oftentimes hunted by Christian neighbors and turned over to the Gestapo for disposal, thus cleansing Poland of its three million Jews.

Comparable incidents occurred elsewhere. In the United States, Britain, and Canada, the discrimination was benign. Signs were posted at summer resorts: "No dogs or Jews allowed." With the defeat of Germany, Italy, Spain, and Japan, a semblance of peaceful order was restored. The United Nations voted for the honoring of the Balfour Declaration assuring Jews status in Palestine. Yet here too the agitations went to work. The wars of '48, '56, '67, '73, the *intifadeh*, the suicide bombers, the chicanery of Arafat and others have kept the kettle burning. Peace, peace, yet no peace. Still worrying and still wondering when the blessed peace assured by the prophets will arrive.

Adonai roi lo echsar

Adonai is my shepherd; I lack nothing (Psalm 23:1).

What a statement! What faith. I remember as a child my father saying to me, "God provides, but you have to pitch in." In this Psalm, David is saying that no matter if you pitch in or not, *Adonai* is there.

It's time we learned that God's presence is forever assured. If our traditions teach us anything, it is that God's love is always there. He's always prepared to take back the stray. No matter what road we may have taken in life, God doesn't stand at the head or the foot of the road and say to you, "You messed up. You took the wrong road." God may raise a quizzical eyebrow and wonder why you did it. But God will never say, "Because you did it, you are condemned." The words of the Psalmist are always with us: "I lack nothing." Whether it be food, health, wealth, or good feeling, all we have to do is look around us, and we'll find the food we need. Search within ourselves, and we'll discover our own inner physician. Sit back and take inventory of our skills, our dreams, and our yearnings, and we'll discover the wealth we need. As for good feelings, all we need is to say to ourselves, "*Adonai* is my shepherd; I lack nothing."

Accounting Error

So all the generations from Abraham to David are fourteen generations; and from David to the deportation to Babylon, fourteen generations; and from the deportation to Babylon to the Messiah, fourteen generations (Matthew 1:17).

Fourteen and fourteen and fourteen make forty-two. If you take the three Hebrew consonants of the name "David" and add their numeric value, D being the fourth letter in the Hebrew alphabet represents 4, W represents 6, so D+W+D = 4+6+4 = 14. Now we understand why the number fourteen may have been important to the Gospel writer. Jesus is portrayed as the son of David, a member of the royal family. But nevertheless, when we count the actual generations listed in the genealogy, the gospel lists forty-one generations only. A simple error; it could have happened to anyone of us.   *DJT*

Mi adameh lakh ... mah ashveh lakh ... mi yirpeh lakh

What shall I attest of you? What is equal to you?
Who shall comfort like you do (Lamentations 2:13)?

Until recent times, "believing" Jews sensed a large divide between themselves and God. No one, they said, can be compared to You. Who is like You? Who can claim the same worth? Who is equal to You? It bordered on anthropomorphism. God and the human can and should be evaluated by common formulas. It led to many personal expressions and personal adorations. In fact, in some of those Jewish communities who paid close attention to folklore, God was seen in the most personal way. God is here; God is there. Many of us still feel that way, still experience God in that most intimate manner. In certain schools of psychology, God is an archetype, as are many other aspects and figures involved in our lives.

If God is an archetype, then God is a universal experience. Thus everyone by nature experiences God. A question, therefore, arises: If God is a universal experience, how do we acknowledge this manifestation? What are the signs or the markings of that experience? In Jewish terms, we would say "when one lives through a moment when he sense it's all together, it all makes sense, it's a God-moment." Or, when one puts aside differences, and instead of a chasm, has a bridge between himself and another, that's a God-moment. Or when one is moved to stretch out his hand to a total stranger and bring him into one's personal orbit, that's a God-moment; or better, a God-moment is when one's separateness is translated to togetherness.

Prayer of a Cancer Patient

I am one who has seen affliction under the rod of God's wrath;
he has driven and brought me into darkness without any light;
against me alone he turns his hand, again and again, all day long.
He has made my flesh and my skin waste away, and broken my bones
(Lamentations 3:1-4).

I am broken. No way out. Why me?   *DJT*

Ve-yivtichu ve-kha yodei shemekha

Those who truly know Your name trust You (Psalms 9:11).

There are many levels of knowing. There is the level of "how do you do? I know you. We were introduced," or the level of "I know that! I've studied, read, and absorbed information. I know it." But then there is the knowing beyond understanding, sometimes called intuitive knowledge, sometimes described as "from my guts." A knowing which requires no proof, nor does it call for experience. It's there; it's as a plain as the nose on your face. We who have experienced God and attest to this fact sense such knowing. Carl Jung was once asked, "Do you believe in God," He answered, "I know." It's beyond understanding. The Psalmist refers to such knowing as "those who know Your name, those who place their trust in You, for they know You are there." Oftentimes we mistake God for someone whose existence is proven. That's not God, nor is it the product of imagination, but it is the product of proof. That's an intellectual exercise. If I address your proof and come up with a counter-proof, then God is no longer a part of our conversation, and God has been disproven.

The God "in whom we trust" is there because we know "this God." Therefore, we place our trust in what we know.

Shomer Yisrael, shemor et shearit Yisrael

O Guardian of Israel, watch over the remnant of Israel
(from the Nefilat Apayim, in the traditional Jewish liturgy).

To be a Jew, and to see oneself as part of the Jewish experience, one must assume certain "truths." By saying "I am a Jew," I am linking myself to a series of historical experiences and a sense a Power greater than the human involved in these experiences. The Power has been known in different periods of time as *El*, *Elohim*, *Shaddai*, or *Adonai*. Each of these names points to various moments and forms of experience. All of them refer to a Power greater than our human selves. At first, it was felt that this Power was the creator of the human, and that creation infused a part of Itself into the human and "the human became a living being." This idea is an essential part of the Jewish psyche. The human, unlike other species or parts of nature, possesses a divine or creator aspect. Outside of the human, the creator exists in the totality of creation. The Jewish experience suggests and teaches that this creator is constantly manifesting itself, sometimes as *El*, the ultimate power or energy of the universe, other times as *Elohim*, the totality of the All that ensures the universe's continuation. If one tampers with that which is the core, or the essence of the universe, than one exposes oneself to a reaction. It can be compared to tampering with gaseous fumes or with electrical wiring. *Shaddai* is that aspect of the creator that brings forth "the rain in its time, the produce in its time, the energy in its needed time." In other words, the creator as constant provider. And finally, *Adonai*, based on the text, "My name *YHWH* (pronounced "*Adonai*" by Jews) was not revealed to them. It is the constant unfolding understanding and knowledge of the creator." From this followed all of the tenets of Jewish mysticism. God is in a constant state of unfolding and becoming. The mystical journey is one that attempts to bring us to the creator, *Adonai*.

Thus the prayer to the keeper of Israel, the one who watches over Israel, is don't abandon them when they call upon you.

Min ha-meitzar qarati Ya, anani be-merchav Ya

From the depth I cried out to God.
He answered me with the breadth of God (Psalms 118:5).

Many times in life, we see ourselves entrapped, as if we are living in an enclosure with no exit, no way out. We cry out, we ask for help, we pray. But the enclosed feeling is still with us. In our despair, we say oftentimes, "This is beyond me. I don't know what is troubling me. Why do I feel enclosed?" We sit, we meditate, we seek a quiet spot, yet we sense the enclosure has not been removed. The Psalmist calls such places *meitzar*. In fact, the Hebrew name for the country (Egypt) where Scripture tells us the Israelites were enslaved (*Mitzrayim*) is the ultimate enclosed space. What were Egypt's halmarks? No space for the Israelites. They were confined to two places: Pithom and Ramses. The ruler of the place was known as Pharaoh—the Abandoner. Thus in *Mitzrayim*, the enclosed land from which none escaped, even in this place, our faith was such that we called to *Adonai*, "Let us no longer be abandoned in this closed land."

But, says the Psalmist, my hope is that you will answer in a wide, open place. It is possible. The Israelites, on leaving Egypt (the enclosed space), were wary of the *midbar*, the open space. Many had said it was a dangerous place, filled with wild beasts and wild fauna. Many feared the *midbar* as dangerous, and therefore wondered, why here? We want the *merchav*, the wide open place. The lesson being, even the *meitzar*, the bad place was still a God-place.

Qarov Adonai le-khol qorav
le-khol asher yiqrauhu be-emet

Adonai is near to all who call upon Him.
He only asks it be done with truth (Psalms 145:18).

What is truth? How can we be assured it is what is claimed for it? The Hebrew word for truth is *emet*. Most recent investigations see *emet* as a shortened form of *emenet*, derived from "amen," meaning *emet* translated as "truth" truly means "firmness" or "faithfulness." Thus the Psalmist is saying that *Adonai* responds to those who are saying what they believe (faith), or better, are firmly convinced of the words they utter. They are on the level of *amen,* if truth be told.

The Psalmist says, "Those who approach or call *Adonai* and do so firmly from a stance of faith receive a response. If the faith you profess isn't a true one, a faithful one, you won't connect (you get only a dial-tone)." This doesn't mean that God ignores the others. It means that God shows us the way out of the morass, the traps laid for us by ourselves and by others. It begins with *emet,* words well spoken, firmly affirmed, that bring the sense of God's presence into our midst. These days, when we are asked to believe what do we know or have arrived at, this affirmation is a healthy antidote to the questionable cures presented by others.

When we, the followers and upholders of our Jewish traditions, consider the question of peace and messianic times, many questions arise. Granted, the pursuance of peace is the ultimate virtue, for we have been taught: "Hillel says, 'Be of

the disciples of Aaron, loving peace and pursuing peace.' "
We ask, "Whom shall we love, how shall we pursue peace?"

The *Avot de-Rabi Natan* answers the question: Among ourselves in the Holy Land and elsewhere, we should pursue peace the way Aaron did. He listened to everyone, he gave credence to both sides of a dispute. He sought opportunities to mediate differences and not exaggerate them. When we are abroad among people who don't possess this Aaronic tradition of being the constant peacemaker, we are told to pursue peace. Seek moments when peace can be arrived at. Shun the turbulence that causes rifts among friends and brings bloodshed among nations. "Seek peace within our place and pursue it to another place."

Adam toeh mi-derekh ha-sekhel be-qehal refaim yanuach

A man who strays from the path of understanding comes to rest in the company of the dead (Prov. 21:16).

"Understanding" in biblical terms means having the capacity to discern, to separate the wheat from the chaff, to know what is essential and what is peripheral, to be able to hone in on any issue and say, "this is the lesson." Thus, if you're walking down the street and you see an animal struggling, don't say to yourself, "If only I had a gun, I'd put it out of its misery." But rather say, might I not take it home, extend love to it, and bring it back so it can stand on its own four feet. *Binah* (understanding) is a special art; it calls for a sensitivity triggered by an experienced situation. It doesn't call for formulas, scientific analysis, or metaphysical speculation. Rather, it calls for a response from the heart, from your intuitive sense, and from whatever compassion you might possess. *Binah* is also used in situations when understanding is called for. For example, if I were a judge and a case came before me, in Jewish terms I'd be expected to judge in an objective way, as the text tells us, "neither inclined to the rich nor to the poor, neither to the powerful nor to the weak." I can tell you from my own experience, during my days of the active rabbinate, that I had to bridle my initial feelings. If someone came into my office and asked for an act of mediation of my part, I had to rid myself of subjective feelings. That's the essence of *binah*.

Ad matai reshaim Adonai
ad matai reshaim yaalozu

How long shall the wicked, O Lord,
how shall the wicked exult (Psalm 94:3)?

We would like to suggest another translation. How long shall
reshaim continue to exist, Adonai? How long will they rejoice?
Reshaim is translated as "wicked"; a *rasha* is the opposite of
tzadiq, a pious, righteous person. The Psalmist and other biblical writers juxtaposed *tzedeq* and *rasha.* The absence of sense
of *tzedeq* brings in its wake an approach which we call *rasha.*
All of us, in our journey through life, have encountered people whom we would gladly place in either category. But every
so often, we encounter individuals who are neither completely one nor the other. They seem to live in a gray area;
neither in the sunlight of *tzedeq* or in the darkness of *rasha.*
Most of our Jewish tradition addresses itself to that gray area.
The people who haven't made up their mind one way or another. Didn't Rabba once say that the *mitzvot* are not needed
by God, but by us humans, to help us to find our way in life,
and possibly reach someday the level of *tzadiq?*

Most times, we neither assign one person or another to either of the two extreme categories of *tzedeq* and *rasha.* For a
question arises: Is it possible to get out of the gray area, and
address ourselves to the possibility of joining the area of
light? Some would say that whenever you perform a *mitzvah,*
you are putting your toe before the foot, into the living waters
of righteousness. You don't have to swim in the whole pool,

you just have to take the chance of placing your toe in the pool. Opportunities for *mitzvot* are legion, from having a smile on a dour day, to helping prepare someone's final rest, from feeding the hungry, to giving advice to a troubled soul; from paying attention to a neglected part of nature (plant, animal, or human), to helping someone across the street. Wherever you turn in life, the opportunity for a mitzvah arises. So, in Judaism, we say "Yes, you can go from the gray to the light."

A Big Ol' Fish Story

Then Jonah prayed to the LORD his God from the belly of the fish, saying, "I called to the LORD out of my distress, and he answered me; out of the belly of Sheol I cried, and you heard my voice. You cast me into the deep, into the heart of the seas, and the flood surrounded me; all your waves and your billows passed over me" (Jonah 2:1-3).

A fish came and swallowed him. Jonah prays, thanking for his miraculous rescue. He prays and prays and prays; and after three days this is too much for the big ol' fish, and he throws up. Some exegetes consider the Book of Jonah a satire, full of irony; the narrator wants to express the opposite of what he or she says. Too pious a prayer can make even a fish puke. *DJT*

Halo atah me-qedem Adonai Elohai qedoshi, lo namut

You, O Lord, are forever.
My holy God, you never die
(Habakuk 1:12).

Habakuk was a man of great faith; we know very little of his life and even less of his ministry. It's a short book, but filled with profound messages. Consider the words we quoted. Why would anyone speak of God as someone who never dies? Obviously, Habakuk was speaking not only to contemporaries but also to the world around. It was filled with dying and born-again gods. In some parts of the Fertile Crescent, there were seasonal ceremonies of the dying and the born-again god, and at these ceremonies, you had to relive the ritual, almost as if each year were a beginning-time again. Our Hebrew biblical tradition quotes this statement of Habakuk in order to let us know that when we speak of God, it's not a seasonal affair. You, God, have been there from time everlasting. When one walks through life with such deep feelings about the eternity of God, one is truly blessed.

Can you imagine? No matter what confronts you, even death, why worry? Some part of you will link up again with the Everlasting. Some might even call it an insurance policy. That's the meaning of faith in Jewish thought, *emunah*, of the same root as the word *amen,* and it means not only "amen" (that's true) but also "amen" (I'm bound, tied, linked, rooted).

Dor le-dor yishabach maasekha u-gevurotkha yagidu.

*Each generation praises Your deeds
and speaks of Your might (Psalms 135:4).*

From one generation to the next, one hears the sounds of
awe and wonder when viewing the world You created. Your
continuous vigor and the telltale marks of Your presence and
existence abounds.

When Ecclesiastes said, "Generations come and go, the
earth is on its axis," I'm sure he was expressing a sense of awe
and wonder. How can it be? What is the secret of a continually surviving universe? We of the faith community of Israel
would say, "The wonder of the universe is its sense of endur-
ance." Earthquakes, destructive fires, and flood come and go,
and yet the universe continues. Even the human mismanage-
ment and devastation of nature hasn't affected its integrity.
True, species have disappeared, yet others have arisen in their
place.

In our studies, we've realized that contained within each of
us is our own curative process, our own inner physician. This
too is part of the awe and the wonder. Seasons come and go,
generations come and go. The assurance of Genesis, of the
regenerative possibilites of all that is and all that will be,
brings hope and peace to us. Every generation lauds Your
deeds, and each in its turn tells us of Your essential strength.
Eternity is the seal, faith is the glue. Together, generations

come and go, and You the Creator are here to remind us of
the truth of the tale told time and again.

Thank God We Are Rich

*You shall not covet your neighbor's house; you shall not covet your
neighbor's wife, or male or female slave, or ox, or donkey, or anything
that belongs to your neighbor (Exodus 20:17).*

Just for a moment consider the possibility the Ten Commandments were not delivered with thunder and lightning,
leaving Moses standing on the mountain, two heavy stone
tablets under his arms. Who could have written them?

Someone who owned a house. A married businessman,
who had men and women working for him, who counted
among his possessions an ox and a donkey, i.e. a truck and a
car. Or do you think an unmarried slave girl would have
asked for this kind of protection?   *DJT*

Harcheq me-shaken ra

Distance yourself from a bad neighbor (Mishnah Avot 1:7).

"Distance yourself from a bad neighbor." It's a broad statement, and can suggest many things. What is a "bad neighbor?" Robert Frost deplored fences, implying they make bad neighbors. Are we to say, therefore, whoever separates himself from us is a bad neighbor? Dennis the Menace of the comicstrips is forever contending with Mr. Wilson. At times, Mr. Wilson seems annoyed with Dennis' antics. Does this dub him with the epithet "bad neighbor?" Or, the cattle-owners of frontier days, whose cattle wandered from field to field, destroying the crops of neighbors, were they bad neighbors? Good and bad have to be defined, their boundaries established.

Everyone seems to agree that the mark of a good neighbor is a caring person, always inquiring about you. The neighbor drops in, seeks your acquaintance, and tries to find areas of mutual interest and possible assistance. A bad neighbor is the indifferent one, who neither cares nor concerns himself about you, often offering the excuse that he doesn't want to intrude into your affairs. The Sage quoted above would say, "The good neighbor is the one who cares, the bad one is the indifferent one."

If only we could adopt this point of view, the fences we seem to experience in life would vanish, and the wide open, welcoming space we seek would appear.

Mamlechet kohanim be-goy qadosh

A kingdom of priests within a holy nation (Exodus 19:6).

Moses, in his final address to his fellow Israelites, describes them as an elect community of *kohanim*, people specially dedicated to the service of Adonai, a community that is *qadosh*, set aside for special living and special purpose.

In the annals of the world, this statement has been labeled the essence of arrogance. How can anyone boast possession of special attributes, special status? To say this in the name of God was hubris, an excess of pride. It's true that we humans do have a tendency to be overly proud, to see ourselves as better than others. For many, it's a defense against insecurity. When this occurs, we oftentimes see it as aberrant behavior. But does this forever preclude the possibility of us saying, "We don't want to be run-of-the-mill. We want to see ourselves as on a journey to higher and higher heights. We don't want to give ourselves the lament of inertia, 'Why bother? Why strive? Why attempt to remedy destructive, self-abnegating behavior?'" We can be more than we are. We want to believe that being human also means being potentially ready and prepared for whatever may confront us, darkness or light, in faith and not in fear.

Seeing ourselves as journeymen, ascending the sacred mountain, prepared to face the winds, the trials, the constant awareness of what might be, we can go forward, and we can face whatever challenges us for good or for ill. That's what being a member of the *qadosh* army implies.

Qedoshim tihiyu
ki qadosh ani Adonai eloheikhem

Be holy, for I the Lord your God am holy (Leviticus 11: 44).

This verse has brought forth endless comments. What is it saying: "You shall be holy?" When? Now? Later? How do I know if I have achieved a holy state? What is holy?

Whenever we seek to understand a biblical verse, we must return to its original language, in this case, Hebrew. It is *qadosh, Q-D-Sh.* The verb means "set aside." Thus, "you shall set yourselves aside, just as I, God, am set aside." Setting aside implies uniqueness. Don't be one of the crowd. Set limits on your instincts. Let them be channeled into constructive and not destructive paths.

This verse is followed by a long list of examples that carry out the *Q-D-Sh* approach, from a weekly day of rest, to avoiding manipulative religious practices. From the honoring of your neighbor's property to the honoring of the concept of family. When approaching life from the standpoint of *qadosh,* family doesn't end with father, mother, sister, brother, or even extended bloodlines, but it includes acquaintances too. For the *qadosh* life is an inclusive one. It can be traced from the arrival of the primeval human on the scene down to the present generation. We are all bound to each other, no matter to what group we may claim membership. Even the stranger among you is under the canopy of *qadosh,* for I, the Creator, see all of you as an extension of Me.

Gam ki eleikh be-geh tzalmavet, lo irah ra

Even though I walk in the valley of the shadow of death, I fear no evil (Psalms 23:4).

Our life consists of peaks and valleys, of shadows and bursting light. We walk through urban and rural centers. Wherever we may be, we experience hills and valleys, or (as the poet would say) hill and vale. One moment we are above it all, in another world, immersed in the essence of the moment. The next moment we are held down below, drowning in an ever increasing flood of worry and cares. Our emotions seem to be cascading from hope to fear, from faith to doubt.

The Psalmist in Psalm 23 continuously sensed this view of reality. At times, it seems he too knew the roller coaster that is life. His response is not despair, defeat, or the abandoning of hope, rather he says, "though I walk in the valley through *geh tzalmavet*, the very valley that reeks with the presence of death, I FEAR NOTHING. No evil, no pain, no despair, for I sense Your (God's) presence." In fact, says the Psalmist, whatever hindrance I encounter ultimately vanishes because of my faith in God's presence.

"You prepare a table for me in the presence of my enemies," it continues. They can no longer deride me or deprive me of my worth, for, says he, I have God at my side, helping me to navigate the shoals, the pits, the traps that confront me in life. Having arrived at a state of inner peace, he reaches a stage of rest and again knows the beauty of life.

*

Most of us seem to be in a hurry. It reminds me of my children in their younger days, asking me every five minutes, "Are we there yet?" We never arrive there. We're only going on the way there. Thus, the lesson should be, don't give in to despair, but look instead for faint glimmers of hope in the dark horizon.

We humans are forever exaggerating our expectations. We haven't learned the first and most important spiritual lesson—patience. To be patient means to be able to say, "Though I may not have what I'm looking for, it doesn't mean it won't ever arrive." Nor should we expect what we're looking for to be the exact duplicate of the image our mind produces.

Many years ago, a young lady came to see me. She was distraught. She had many hopes and dreams, and she believed that if she so hoped, or dreamt, someone out there would guarantee the fulfillment of her hopes and dreams. If she so willed it, so it must be. She never learned the lesson of patience, nor the lesson that dreams sometimes are fulfilled in many forms, many of which we never visualize. If you and I dream of something, the energy the dream implies may arrive in a form other than the one we expected. The *Ethics of the Fathers* teaches, "*al tistaqel be-kankan eleh mah she-yesh bo*"—never judge a book by its cover, nor evaluate the contents of a vessel by the vessel itself. The fact that the vessel is pretty doesn't mean the contents are worth embracing.

va-yipach be-apav

And (God) blew into his nose (or nostrils) (Genesis 2:7).

How shall we read a text? Any text, sacred or secular. I have come to the conclusion that all of life is a metaphor. As a popular tune would say, life isn't what it seems to be. Jewish and Christian traditions said about texts, "Don't see them as literal statements. Each text points to many levels." Every life points to many levels. If I'm told a story, I ask, "What's behind it?" I ask this without rendering any judgment.

Being a Jungian in my psychological understanding, I always feel that each moment, each act, points to another. It's a form of *qabalah* mysticism: One is always in a state of becoming; one is never there. The moment is in and of itself, yet it is also a stepping stone toward another. All of this is an outgrowth of my understanding of the phrase in Genesis/Bereshit: *va-yipach be-apav.* The Creator inserted in the original human, the *anthropos,* a breath that was not an ordinary breath, a wind, a breeze, but a *neshamah,* a divine or spiritual breath transforming the *anthropos* into a living being, one who is able to see beyond the moment, who is aware of something waiting to be discovered and identified.

Ve-ruach Elohim merachefet al-pinei ha-mayim. This phrase is translated many ways. One of the most popular is, "And the Spirit of the Lord floated over the face of the Deep." Is this all we can say about pre-Creation? The spirit or the wind of God hovered? What is the spirit? Is it a part of the pre-Creation scene that exists no more, or, as the verse implies, was it an inherent part of the pre-Creation scene that survived into post-Creation. From the text, we feel the scene included an undefined mass, and the spirit hovered over it. From the text, it would seem this spirit was a seeding device, and its energy affected the unchartered chaos. Many have thought that the spirit was an emanation of the Creator, not the Creator itself. The Creator cannot be defined, therefore the Creator has many names, each one describing another aspect of the Creator.

But the question isn't totally resolved. What does *mirachefet*, hovering, truly mean? *Mirachefet* has a floating quality about it; it is here, it is there. It is without bounds, it is without position. This floating Spirit is a part of Creation, as is every aspect of the act. For this Spirit is always present, available, forever acting as a guide and compass. When we human tamper with the Creation, change its aspect, then the Spirit brings it back. Thus, the biblical tradition states, "The world will never cease to exist, denying the crying and whining of the Apocalypse."

Sex and the City

(Song of Songs 1:5-7).

I am black and beautiful, O daughters of Jerusalem.
Do not gaze at me because I am dark, because the sun has gazed on me.

Beautiful women of the City, look at me! My skin is tanned from the sun and your envious looks do not bother me.

They made me keeper of the vineyards,
but my own vineyard I have not kept!

I am a country girl. But I am not a virgin.

Tell me, you whom my soul loves, where you pasture your flock, where
you make it lie down at noon; for why should I be like one who is veiled
beside the flocks of your companions?

Where do you break for lunch, my lover? Where can we meet? My body is beautiful, why should I not show it?   *DJT*

Otem azno me-zaakat dal
gam hu yiqra ve-lo yaaaneh

If a man shuts his ears to the cry of the poor,
he too will cry out and not be answered (Proverbs 21:13).

Modern scandal is the excuse that people give for disregarding the poor, the forgotten, the neglected. "If only they would pull themselves up by their bootstraps, all would be well." "If only they weren't so lazy, all would be well." Our tradition tells us that the poor will never vanish from the land. It's the nature of the beast. Some are stronger than others, some are more physically adept than others, some come into this life better physically endowed than others. You can't point your finger at individuals who may not be on top of the endowment scale and act as if they don't exist. If there's one poor person in this world, then every one of us has an obligation to care for that person and to include him in the family that is humankind. Our tradition tells us not only to provide for the less fortunate, but also try to create a situation for that person so that he may become a productive member of society (cf. Maimonides). I would suggest that we teach our children quite early Maimonides' Eight Stages of *Tzedaqah* (Righteous Living). In my youth, my father ingrained in me a principle of *matan be-seiter*, giving without public acknowledgement. He said, you don't give or share because of the accolades you might receive, but rather by letting your heart be your guide, and responding to whatever you see around you in need of *tiqun olam*, universal repair.

Not a Word To Say

Now there was a great outcry of the people and of their wives against
their Jewish kin.
For there were those who said, "With our sons and our daughters, we
are many; we must get grain, so that we may eat and stay alive."
There were also those who said, "We are having to pledge our fields, our
vineyards, and our houses in order to get grain during the famine."
And there were those who said, "We are having to borrow money on our
fields and vineyards to pay the king's tax. Now our flesh is the same as
that of our kindred; our children are the same as their children; and yet
we are forcing our sons and daughters to be slaves, and some of our
daughters have been ravished; we are powerless, and our fields and
vineyards now belong to others."
I was very angry when I heard their outcry and these complaints.
After thinking it over, I brought charges against the nobles and the
officials; I said to them,
"You are all taking interest from your own people."
And I called a great assembly to deal with them, and said to them, "As
far as we were able, we have bought back our Jewish kindred who had
been sold to other nations; but now you are selling your own kin, who
must then be bought back by us!"

They were silent, and could not find a word to say
(Nehemiah 5:1-8).

The citizens of a town organized a protest march to City Hall.
"First we had to go in debt just to provide for the basic
needs of our family: food, clothes, housing, health care,

transportation, and tuition."

"Then our companies were downsized and most of us were laid off. We had to refinance our homes but the economy did not improve."

"And when tax-day came we were criminalized, because we had no cash."

"Our children are moving away," a mother yelled into the megaphone. "They work three jobs in the big city just to make ends meet. My daughter is molested by her boss, and there is nothing we can do about it!"

The mayor of the city was outraged.

He summoned the rich families of the town and the official representatives of the local banks, of the credit card companies, of the factories, and of the local university. He made them stand in front of the crowd.

"Were you not born and raised in the same town as these people?" the mayor asked. "We worked hard to make this town a better place. And yet you are forcing our young people to move away! And while you live off the interest of your own kin you expect charities to raise money to feed them!"

The rich families and the officials were silent and could not find a word to say.   *DJT*

Shomer Yisrael shmor shearit Yisrael ha-omrim Shema Yisrael

*O guardian of Israel, stand watch over the remnant of Israel,
those who say "Shema Yisrael"*
(from the Nefilat Apayim *in the traditional liturgy).*

As a believing Jew, I've never felt abandoned. Alone, yes—
abandoned, no. For the verse in Psalm 27 says, "My father
and mother may abandon me, but I know You, God, are
there."

In fact, I deeply believe in the Jewish mission, namely, to
bring as many as I may know to the mountain where all are
one: brothers, sisters, fathers, mothers, sons, and daughters,
and the rest of the kinfolk.

Where is that mountain? Does it have a specific location?
How do we even know it exists? We know. Every so often,
we see someone gravitating to another person. We sense a
stretching out of one hand to another. Not the kind of
stretching out you find within a closed group, but in the lar-
ger, wider, and more extensive world.

We humans by nature are lonely creatures. Our mothers
give birth to us, but then the umbilical cord is cut, and we are
left to our own devices. It's true, we have teachers, guides,
and others. But though we have them, we don't necessarily
absorb their advice and guidance. We contain within ourselves self-censors that pick and choose what seems to fit in
with our worldview and ignore the rest. Our ancient teachers
advised us to behave accordingly. Don't consider only one

vessel, rather regard its contents. Or discard the shell and accept its kernel.

But one thing we know deep in our hearts, even in a lonely
moment, is that there is the refuge of God. Keeper of Israel,
Guardian of Israel's remnants, let not those who dearly profess their linkage to you (*ahav* = love = linkage) feel abandoned. For you are the One who brought us all to life. Help
us remain in life.

Shokhen ad marom ve-qadosh shemo

The One who dwells in every corner of the universe is way beyond us, and His name is Qadosh, the sacred one
(from Pesuqei de-Zimra *for Shabbat in the traditional liturgy).*

This phrase begins the weekly *Shabbat* service. It's telling us that the God to whom we are addressing ourselves lives all over the place, and you realize His presence by the *qadosh,* the distinctiveness, that is He. No one can give us a map that will bring us to a specific place where *Adonai* dwells. As I've said in a previous piece, He's all over. The entire universe is suffused with His presence. In order for you to realize this, you must begin by saying, "Yes, it's true. God exists." You may ask, "If that's so, why can't I find Him?" The answer is simple. Our Jewish tradition tells us that everyone has a purpose in life. The ultimate mission is to be a *malakh* (angel) of *Adonai,* whose assignment is to become the presence of God for some specific person. If your life has been anything like mine, I'm sure you realize that people appear on your horizon unannounced; they are complete strangers to you, and yet they have something to say or do that turns your life around. And you stand in awe. Where did he or she come from? Why are his or her words so familiar? What's he or she trying to say? And when you take a step back, you think and sit quietly, and it suddenly dawns on you that it was serendipitous. This person had to come to you in order for you to reach your own state of wholeness. And that's what *qadosh* means: it's what makes you distinct from another, and *Shabbat,* the day of the great exercise of discovery, of who you are, what you are, why you are here, goes into full gear.

Ivdu et Adonai be-simchah

Serve Adonai with simchah (Psalm 35:2).

Some translate *simchah* as joy, but it means more. *Simchah* is a state, a soul-state. It is a state of being when all parts of you are involved, when you feel you have turned yourself over to another, when you place yourself at another's footstool and say, "I am Yours. Take me into Your very being." As the text tells us, the ultimate way of serving God is to bring every part of me to the point where in my totality, I say: *"Mi chamokhah? Who is like You, O God?"* *Simchah* is the ultimate universal state, when everything is together, where there are no reservations and no ifs, ands, or buts get in the way. It's the state wherein I can say, "I know God exists. I know He is always with me. I know He doesn't condemn me, and he appreciates my human dilemma and realizes that ofttimes whatever I do is but an outgrowth of my human chemistry." When I serve God with *simchah*, then hate disappears, jealousy vanishes, selfishness is placed on a back burner, and I am ready to sing, to laugh, to dance, to be filled with all that helps me say, "How glorious is the world in which we live!"

Satan

The LORD said to Satan, "Have you considered my servant Job?
There is no one like him on the earth, a blameless and upright man who
fears God and turns away from evil." (Job 1:8)

My four-year-old stepson woke up in the middle of the night, crying. He had seen the devil in his dream. I tried to comfort him and told him that there was no devil, and that the devil only existed in stories.

He asked me, "And what do I do if the devil comes out of the story?"   *DJT*

Amein

(Said by the congregation in response to many prayers.)

Many have wondered, from where does *Amein* stem? It is an acronym for *El Melekh Neeman.* God is a reliable ruler. Why do we believe this? After all, if many of the criticisms of God are correct, if God at times is unjust or judgmental, how can you say He is reliable? You don't know what His next move may be. Furthermore, if God is reliable, and He is in every corner of the universe, why can't we accurately predict and control all that happens in this universe? You say our knowledge of God is limited. Since He is *Ein Sof,* endless, how can you therefore pinpoint Him? Whatever part of Him you may describe is only partial. Being *Ein Sof,* you can only catch a glimpse of Him, as Scripture tell us about Moses' experience with God. He caught a glimpse of God, only saw a part of Him. Perhaps our measuring tools are incorrect. Perhaps we are measuring God as we would any visible item; but if we believe and say that God is all-pervasive, wherever you turn He is there, then how can you measure God as you would any measurable item? Perhaps when we speak of God, we are speaking of Something beyond all human phenomena. In our Jewish tradition, God is known as *Ha-maqom,* the Place, Something that is always there, like home, like the solid rock on which your true residence is built. It's always there, It always awaits you, It's not something to which you return, but rather something that you never leave. If that is so, then it can be said: *El (God) Melekh Neeman,* is truly there, never vanishes, never disappears, and is always there.

Barukh atah be-mevoekha barukh atah be-tzeitekha

You are blessed in your coming and in your going (Deutoronomy 28:6).

When are we blessed? When is the blessing real and genuine? When is an incident a pseudo-blessing? What is the earmark of a blessing?

The word *barukh* is related to *B-R-Kh,* the word for "knees." When one seeks a relationship with someone, one shows deference. We bow, we bend our knees, we kneel. So when we say *barukh atah,* you are in possession of a *B-R-Kh.* When you arrive and when you leave, we are saying you have reached the status of *berekh* (relationship). The relationship is firm, established. When I say "I feel *berekh,*" it is more than a recognition of a physical state. It's an overwhelming feeling: I am no longer part of an undefined mass, a bubble in a sea of soap-suds. I'm defined; I'm almost ensconced. There is a uniqueness, a distinctiveness that is me. I am protected by a power greater than I have ever known. This feeling is with me when I arrive and when I leave. It's always there.

You may ask, "But how do I achieve it? I'd like to assure myself with such status." First, it calls for a specific state of mind. No longer should you feel a state of isolation, but now you can enjoy a state of connectedness. Second, that relationship with the one who I think has extended to me the sense of *B-R-Kh* is based on trust. I trust him or her, therefore it's possible for me to achieve a sense of *B-R-Kh* with him or her. Third, once I've received the sense of *B-R-Kh*, then all is in place. Guilt is gone; *should have*, *would have* are meaningless, for I am in the moment, and in a true relationship that is *B-R-Kh*.

And The Word Becomes Flesh

In the night I saw a man riding on a red horse! He was standing among the myrtle trees in the glen;
and behind him were red, sorrel, and white horses.
Then I said, "What are these, my lord?"
The angel who talked with me said to me, "I will show you what they are" (Zechariah 1:7-10).

The Word of God becomes flesh through interpretation. *DJT*

Mekalkel chayim be-chesed, mechayeh meitim be-rachmamim rabim

*You are the one that nourishes the living with kindness and revives the
dead with great compassion
(from the* Amidah *in the traditional liturgy).*

Chesed and *rachamim* are two central concepts in Judaism. *Chesed* is translated as "lovingkindness" and *rachamim* as "compassion." Let's consider the entire phrase. Speaking of God, it says, "He [God] graciously grants and gives the gift of *chayim*, life." None of us can assume that life in all its connotations and manifestations is ours. Today, we are here; tomorrow, we are gone. Each day is an act of grace, extended to us, the recipients. Our tradition carries this thought to another plane: the same One who extends life with grace, also extends eternal life with compassion. It is an answer to those who insisted that life after death is prompted by harsh judgment. If you behave *x*, this is your reward; if you behave *y*, this is your punishment. The above-quoted phrase implies such standards that aren't part of our outlook. Compassion, loving kindness, and love is the earmark of our relationship to *Adonai*. Thus, *ve-ahavta*, you shall love the Lord your God, your *rea*, your neighbor, as yourself. The Hebrew word *ahav* (love) in its fullest sense means "link." You shall be *linked* to your friend as your are *linked* to yourself. You shall be *linked* to Adonai unconditionally. Note, this linkage does not differentiate between God and any other kind of friend. Try for whoever and whatever is closest to you to establish a relationship of linkage, since the entire universe is linked one part to another. Metaphorically speaking, all of nature is *linked*. No special value is assessed to any part of it, saying one linkage is better than another, one species (plant, animal, human) is better than another.

*Al tivtichu bindivim
be-ven adam she-ein lo teshuah.*

Don't rely on princes, on people *who can't really help you
(Psalms 146:3).*

The major human fallacy lies in the belief that political and public power is an absolute assurance of omnipotence. In my lifetime, public officials ran governments while serving time in jail. Public officials proclaimed one thing when they knew the true facts were otherwise. Scientists have been accused of doctoring up research results, and politicians of manufacturing documents. Thus, the fact that someone occupies a prominent seat in any institution is no guarantee of his or her competence, power, integrity, or effectiveness.

The problem of vain promises, of inflated statements, and of dreams being seen as reality is as old as the human condition. When we are young, we believe in giants; in middle age, we fear ghosts; and in our dotage, we wonder who's standing at the edge of our bed, possibly beckoning to us.

When the Psalmist said, "Don't rely on princes," he or she was referring to people who have crowned themselves with tokens of power. After all, they are *nedivim*. The Psalmist uses the verb *N-D-V* (*nadav*) to signify powerful people, but we suspect its usage to be euphemistic or ironic-"powerful" indeed. Prove it, that you do have the means for *yeshua* (salvation). The mere fact that you are a public official or a high priest doesn't mean anything. What kind of person are you and what path are you on? This is the true question.

Broken Promises?

Lo, I will send you the prophet Elijah before the great and terrible day of the LORD comes. He will turn the hearts of parents to their children and the hearts of children to their parents, so that I will not come and strike the land with a curse (Malachi 4:5-6).

These are the last words of the Christian Old Testament. Reborn Elijah will come and make the unlikely happen: peace between parents and their children, peace between children and their parents.

The Jesus of the Gospels proclaims, "From now on five in one household will be divided, three against two and two against three; they will be divided: father against son and son against father, mother against daughter and daughter against mother, mother-in-law against her daughter-in-law, and daughter-in-law against mother-in-law" (Luke 12:52-53). *DJT*

Barchi nafshi et Adonai
ve-khol qerovai et shem qadsho

Bless the Lord, O my soul,
all my being, His holy name (Psalms 103:1).

From childhood, even in moments of doubt, I've always heard a voice inside of me that said, "Bless the Lord, O my soul, all my being, His holy Name." I've made it my business in the last twenty or thirty years to pull away from the drama and despair of life from time to time and read this psalm. Somehow or another, it gives me hope and faith. It assures me of the forgiveness of my sins and misdeeds, and of the healing of all disease. The Psalmist actually says, "He satisfies you with good things in the prime of life, so that your youth is renewed like the eagles." That's the power of faith, the power that comes to you when you can sit or lie quietly and say, "It's beyond me; therefore I place my body in your hands and my spirit, too. *Adonai* is with me; I am not afraid." To have that feeling course through your very life helps you see verdant fields where you sense that there might be thorns and thistles. It helps you look at the rose and see it in all its beauty and set aside the fact that there are thorns on its stem. It helps you see the bit of light that breaks through a dark cloud, and quiets you when you hear troubling sounds. Bless *Adonai* my soul, and let every part of me affirm his sacred name.

*

Continuing our discussion of Psalm 19: In Jewish tradition, great emphasis is placed on the concept of *Torah*. The word itself is the derivative of the verb YRH, *yaroh*. According to the Brown-Driver-Briggs lexicon, *yaroh* means "to throw or shoot." A secondary meaning is to "direct or instruct." The term *torah* was given to a special kind of instruction, the instruction of at first the priests who served in the Temple, then second the rabbis who studied in the academies, and later, the discoverers of the secrets of the universe. So, the Psalmist says to us, *torat Adonai temimah, mishivat nafesh*: "The *Torah* of God is pure, it soothes the soul," meaning of course that in this body of information, which we feel comes from nowhere, perhaps like the dream mentioned in the last installment that breaks through the darkness of the night, enlightening the beholder. Thus we would say that all deep knowledge is considered by the Psalmist, and all his spiritual descendants come from God. It's there for consoling, soothing, and (as he says later on) even makes those who are slow in understanding wise.

This Psalm can be considered as part of the Wisdom Literature (the latter part of the Hebrew Bible). Let's look at it carefully. We find some of the most interesting phrases ever contained in Scripture here. For instance, "Day to day makes utterance, night to night speaks out"; the Hebrew is not as clear as the translation would suggest; it reads *yom le-yom yabia omer, ve-leilah le-leilah yechaveh daat*. If we are to literally translate the phrase *yechaveh daat*, it would mean "brings knowledge to life." Therefore, nighttime is the most creative time of the day, for in the night, when one might least expect any profound discoveries, the text would have us believe in the deepest, the most spiritual sense, true wisdom comes forth when we least expect it, when we are not awake, but in deep slumber. The next verse says, *ein omer,* there is no utterance, *ve-ein devarim,* and no words, and yet something comes out during the night, *bli nishmah qolam,* without articulation by our voices. The Psalmist is bringing to us a deep understanding of dreams. In dreams lies deep information. One must never assume that they are foolish statements, not to be regarded seriously. If anything, perhaps they contain greater wisdom than any considerations during the waking hours, for it is in the privacy of the night, the privacy of our inner selves, that we really discover who we are, and perhaps we can carry this interpretation a step further. The Psalmist is saying that this inner statement is greater than the inner statements you hear in the marketplace, the public square, and in community halls. In our time, when we so deride the power of the individual, when we so demand that we all march to the same drum, and when we so flippantly say, "If you disregard the words of a leader, no matter what your soul may say, you are a traitor."

*

Noah was a *tzadiq*, a righteous man in his generation. This statement led to a *talmudic* debate. Rabbi Yochanan said, "If Noah had lived in any other generation, he would have been considered an ordinary man." Resh Lakish said, "Anyone who has the moral strength to rise above his generation, the society in which he lives, is to be commended and considered a righteous person for all times."

This debate is reminiscent of the nature-versus-nurture debate of our times. Some have said that we are what we are because of who we are. Each of us is a self-contained world with the potential for extraordinary greatness. Others have said that society shapes us.

From our knowledge of human psychology, we would say that, in the course of time, our unique sense of self develops, and it is this sense that stands up to our ego's constant search for ways to help us "fit in" to the world as a whole.

Ultimately, it would seem Scripture would have us believe that it is our own sense of self, who we are, what we are, and what we can be, that is the most decisive factor.

Va-tishacheit ha-aretz lifnei Elohim va-timalei ha-aretz chamas. Va-yare Elohim et ha-aretz ve-hineh nishchatah ki hishchit kol basar et darko al ha-aretz. Va-yomer Elohim le-Noach: "Qetz kol basar ba lifanai kil malah ha-aretz chamas mifneihem ve-hinni mashchitam et ha-aretz."

God looked at the earth; it was corrupt, for corrupt were the ways of all life on earth. God said to Noah: "I have decided that the end has come for all living things, for the earth is full of lawlessness because of them. Therefore, I am about to destroy them and the earth"
(Genesis 6:11).

This text vacillates from the wondrously created man and the human's proclivity for *ra kol ha-yom* bad, every day of his life. Why is the human so described, without redeeming features? What flows through the human, producing this bad end-product? "The earth was filled with violence, with lawlessness." It had reverted to its original chaotic state. Thus, we have 6:5–8. God regrets the creation of the human, and 6:11–13, God's plan is that everything will be destroyed. The entire atmosphere has been affected. The bad pervades; it has even infiltrated the ranks of the tamed and untamed beasts of the world. But the Creator hasn't given up completely. He has sentenced to death all existing life except for Noah, for as his name implies, the "bad" never entered his door; it only rested there. With Noah, the spread is contained. He is placed in the sacred vessel, and he later emerges with the fowl and cattle—

animals of all sorts—to start life and civilization again. At first, it rained forty days and forty nights: "The waters swelled on the earth for one hundred and fifty days. Forty days later, Noah opened the window of the ark. At first, a raven was sent; it returned, and the dove followed it. It too returned. Seven days later, the dove was sent out again. At nightfall, the dove returned with an olive leaf in its beak. Seven days later, Noah sent the dove out again, but this time it didn't return." Noah and all of the inhabitants of the ark emerged. Noah sent an offering, a sacred gift, to *Adonai*. *Adonai* is affected by Noah's sense of devotion. *Adonai* said, "No longer will I seek perfection, for the human has a *ra*, a bad streak in itself." He promises never again to seek the destruction of the human or of any creature that inhabits the earth. In this passage, the constant struggle of good and evil is articulated.

New Year's Resolutions

*He blotted out every living thing that was on the face of the ground,
human beings and animals and creeping things and birds of the air; they
were blotted out from the earth. Only Noah was left, and those that were
with him in the ark. ... Then he waited another seven days, and sent
out the dove; and it did not return to him any more. In the six hundred
first year, in the first month, on the first day of the month, the waters
were dried up from the earth; and Noah removed the covering of the ark,
and looked, and saw that the face of the ground was drying
(Genesis 7:23; 8:12-13).*

A story, a story! God saw that men and women were no
good. So God killed them. With the exception of one family,
one couple from every species of animals, and the fish, God
killed all life forms. And when it was over, He saw that men
and women were no better than before, and God decided to
never do it again. It happened on New Year's Day. Who said
God cannot change God's mind? Who said God does not
kill?   *DJT*

Hineh mah tov u-mah naim
shevet achim gam yachad

How good it is
for brothers to rally for each other (Psalms 133:1).

We Jews have always felt a nexus between us and fellow Jews, and between us and humankind. We always said that survival requires a relationship to all that is and all that will ever be. You can't march through life unconcerned, unrelated, and uninvolved in the world that surrounds you. You can close all the windows in your house, but somehow there will still be a whiff of air. You can draw all the shades in your possession, closing out the scenery that surrounds you, but somehow the pollen finds a way to disturb you. You can never say to yourself or to anyone else that "Oceans separate me from the rest of the world" because the water, sooner or later, will touch your shores. The beauty of life lies not in its separateness, but in its togetherness, and the hope of life is not fulfilled when one is oblivious to life beyond oneself.

We've never been able to live peacefully with isolationists. Too often, they remind us of the people living in their own world, unaware that there are worlds beyond their own. Genetics teaches us that all is interrelated, science teaches us all is interrelated, and politics warns us that if we are not interrelated, then chaos will ensue.

kol de-avid rachmana le-tav avid

Whatever God does is for a good purpose (Talmud Berakhot 60b).

In Judaism, in its view of life, God plays a central role. Not only is He the Creator and the Sustainer of the universe, He is the ultimate point in existence. We therefore sometimes wonder, "Does God know what He is doing?" Many times, in moments of despair, we shout "God, Why me?!" or better, in historical moments, "Where were You when we needed You?!" Some of us even go so far as to say, "God doesn't exist; otherwise, he would have prevented the Holocaust." Previously, we've dealt with this question, my point being that humans usually dig their own graves. We can't blame God for our human missteps, nor can we blame God for our blindness and prejudice that prevented us from addressing troubling situations. God is the Power, but that doesn't mean we are powerless. God makes for salvation, but that doesn't mean we are not involved. I've always considered God and humans to be in tandem; when you're on the seesaw, you can't expect to ascend or descend without the aid of a partner. The same is true for what's happening around us and within us. God is the partner, but we are the participants. So when we say, "Whatever God does, there is meaning behind it" and that God is not what some people claim—a vengeful, unforgiving being. To believe in God means to also see yourself in this I-Thou relationship, the relationship of God to man and man to God.

Palgei mayim lev melekh be-yad Adonai al kol asher yachpotz yatenu

In the hand of the Lord, a king's heart is a watercourse;
He directs it wheresoever he pleases (Proverbs 21:1).

Jewish tradition has always taught: From the beginning of the universe until its present day, a universal factor has run through it. It is known as *yad Adonai*, the hand of God. It applied to all. From its inception, Judaism differed from all of the nations that surrounded us Jews by saying that royalty, by its nature, is subject to the same rules as all human beings. We saw this in the story of David and the prophet Nathan, when the prophet tried to tell David that what is forbidden for others is also forbidden for you, and what is expected from others is also expected of you. Too often we find in daily life that people's titles and stations go to their heads, as if to say that there's one set of rules for them and another for the others. We Jews say no; the democracy that law speaks of applies to the old and the young alike, to the powerful and to the weak. Therefore, the *Torah* says, don't play favorites in your lawcourts. Shun bribes, political pressure, and those who think they can buy their way into the congresses or the parliaments of most countries. We in the United States have been faced with the scandals of lobbyists, as if to say, if you have underwritten someone in political office, you're entitled to special privileges. Proverbs says, "The king's heart is in the hand of the Lord" not in the hand of the lobbyist.

One fine day, Abram, a man advanced in age, heard a voice. It said, "Leave." *Lekh lekha*—Go back to yourself. Find out who you are, and let Me guide you to the land that will be yours and that of your descendants. Abram responds to the call. He isn't sure about his future. The call said, "go to the land to which I will direct you. I assure you a great future awaits you and your posterity.

Abram, the believer, the responder to the voice, goes, leaves, knowing he'll be led to the place best suited for him. For he had been told *Lekh lekha*—Go back to yourself. It was a fitting message, for the entire Scriptural saga began with the human who had an implant of sorts, the breath of God that distinguished him from all other beasts of creation, wild or tame. Abram wasn't sure of the phrase "go back to yourself." Who is this "self?" How will I recognize it? How will I ever know if I have truly met it? He was a man of deep trust, however, so he took his chances.

Being told, "I will assign this land to your offspring," he felt reassured, so he traveled the length and breadth of Canaan. He suffered first the attempted liaison of the Pharaoh with his wife, Sarai, then the adventures of his nephew, Lot. He saw the internecine warfare of the valley of Sodom, experienced the Dead Sea, affected his rescue of Lot. But Abram survived the ultimate test, the tempting greed that comes from conquering another. He refused to partake of the looted wealth, nor would he be part and parcel of the enslavement, degradation, and abuse of the prisoners of war. His response, "I will not take so much as a thread or a sandal-strap of what is yours; you shall not say it is I who made Abram rich." He was deserving of chosenness. Thus God says to him, "Fear not, Abram. I am a shield for you. Your reward shall be very great indeed (Genesis 15:1)."

How Jesus Became Christ

An account of the genealogy of Jesus the Messiah (Matthew 1:1).

The first words of the Four-Gospel-Book are: *Biblos* = book, *geneseos* = of the genesis, *Iesou Christou* = of Jesus Christ, or translated into more palatable English: A book about how Jesus became Christ.   *DJT*

Mah she-yaaseh ha-zeman lo yaaseh ha-sekhel

That which time accomplishes, the mind cannot do.

The great healer in Jewish tradition is time. In fact, we're told *ein dochkin et ha-qetz*, you cannot force the arrival of Final Times, as if to say, all that exists in this world has its own time-clock, and it ill behooves us to tamper with it.

Many times, we feel we are at the end of our tether. We don't understand what's going on. We cry, we complain, we seek targets to blame, we seldom say to ourselves, "Sit quietly. Let time be the healer." When we learn that lesson in life, i.e., that the great healer time and the concomitant notion that everything in nature has its own time-clock, we find ourselves moving beyond anxiety and into the lap of calmness and relaxation.

We humans, despite our sophistication, cultivation, and civilization, too often neglect the true lessons which we've inherited from generations past, the greatest of which is *"mah she-yaaseh ha-zeman, lo yaaseh ha-sekhel"* the most sophisticated gameplans can never match.

You may say to me, "Granted, I accept your premise. But how do I change?" Whatever I do in life is prompted by *sekhel*, by reason! Physicians daily tell me that one prescription is better than another, since in trial runs the success rate was higher. Yet the wisest physicians we know will tell us that all colds take seven days, one week, to be cured, no matter what medication you imbibe or swallow. The wise people of this earth are not necessarily the sophisticates. In fact, many of us are beginning to believe that the closer we are to nature, the wiser we may become. So, throughout the world in societies less sophisticated than ours, you will find the wisest among them often are the illiterates who have not accepted culture and wisdom as their own bible, but seek their answers in nature itself.

In the Sabbath liturgy, we find the phrase *tzamah lekha nafshi.* "My soul thirsts for You." Our Sages teach, "The world at creation time found its culmination and fulfillment on *Shabbat.*" It was that day on which *Adonai* rested from His labors and had a *nefesh*-moment, a soul-moment. Thus, in Jewish tradition *Shabbat* is considered the soul-day. There are many terms used in Hebrew for "soul": *nefesh, ruach, neshamah.*

The question of soul—What is a soul?—What levels of souls exist? Which is of higher caliber than the others? What is the purpose of the soul in the human journey? All these questions and many more are discussed in the mystical literature of Judaism. It's main source is the *Zohar.* The *Zohar* teaches that by nature, all souls are pure. No matter what an individual may or may not do, its soul is pure. At times, the bearer of the soul acts to its detriment. He or she overflows with anger, hate, fear—all negative and potentially destructive qualities. Such beings cannot contribute to the one activity for which we are made, namely, to mend the world.

We Jews are taught from our first day on Earth that the world in which we find ourselves is in need of constant repair. It's a given—although our Torah tells us that God's judgment of His creation was "It is good." Nevertheless, by our behavior as human beings, we allow the negative, the corrosive, the destructive tendencies of human behavior and life to prevail. Our excuses are legion, and chief among them is the need to defend ourselves from threatened attack. Our God (Gods) urges us to behave that way, it's incumbent upon us to protect ourselves from that which threatens our existence. Seldom do we observe ourselves to say, "He or she possesses a good soul, a pure soul." Being forever poised in a defensive way, in a protective stance, we feel it is our duty to destroy that which may destroy us, instead of saying "I'll confront or attempt to placate the erstwhile enemy." We therefore have been given the gift of *Shabbat* to help us meet these destructive bodies that seek to destroy rather than build in life.

Ritzon re-av yaseh

We spoke of awe as being one of the feelings we encounter in God-present moments. We spoke of the wonder entailed in an awe-moment. We spoke of the feeling of being on another plane when the awe-experience occurs. At times, in a moment of awe, we feel detached or outside of the orbit of most people we know. Many times, in moments of awe, we feel rootless, perhaps floating on air. The psalmist says that at such moments *Adonai* appears on the scene, and knowing what brings us to this state of awe, responds to the needs, desires, hopes, and wishes of the awe-experience. The Hebrew verb is *yaaseh*, which means "acts, does, responds." The verb is used sparingly in the biblical text. It's used when the acts of creation are reviewed. It isn't just a description of God-accomplishments, but also of God-acts. Acts over which we sometimes wonder in our awestruck "How is this possible? How can this be? It's nothing short of a sign (another word for miracle)!" It is something that neither I nor anyone else can expect, yet it happened, for God did it. Not a human voice, but a God-voice.

Regarding *Elohim*. We translate the word as "God." According to the rabbis of the Talmud and the Midrash, *Elohim* is the god of justice. Just as we know God in his merciful state, we know God in his just state. This led to many commentators saying that, from the beginning, God wanted the universe to be built on a system of justice. Thus, in Deuteronomy 16:20, you find the statement *tzedeq tzedeq tirdof* (pursue justice). An unjust society is a candidate for self-destruction. It is no longer participating in a dialog. No one can survive in isolation, whether he or she be a dictator or a lonely human being. Therefore, in creating the universe, God made sure that it was resting on a platform of justice, of dialog. A successful dialog is a product of mutual respect. I will dialog with you if I'm convinced that you are willing to dialog with me. If we place barriers or if we are dishonest in the exercise, i.e., if I entered into dialog with reservations, it cannot succeed. If I insist that greater consideration be given to me, for whatever the reason may be, it cannot succeed.

The justice dialog urged by the Torah (Scripture) has its own set of values: 1) Everyone must be treated equally, rich or poor; 2) Judges who take sides, politically or otherwise, cannot be part of the system.

The Bible regales us with a strange story. The divine beings were enticed by human beauty and took wives from among them. The text implies that since the divine and the human have comingled, their offspring will not be privy to the ancient promise of eternal life. The implication here is that one cannot be both divine and human at the same time. This has raised many questions. First, if the human and the divine are separate entities, what is the nature of the human spiritual journey? Can we humans ever become other than what we are now? What is meant by nirvana? What is meant by transcendence? What is meant by the notion of being both human and divine, and is such a state of existence possible?

Some will say the Scripture known as the Old Testament (or, as we call it, the Hebrew Bible) has been superceded by the New. Can this be true? After all, we find in the New continuous use of *midrashim*, the products of rabbinic minds and rabbinic interpretation of the Hebrew text. Can it be that an ancient bridge was formed long ago, and that an effort was made to answer the question "Where does the human end and the divine begin?" The Qabalists teach that we are all on a journey (cf., Sky, H. *My Journey*, [2003]). All of us are destined to pass through impediments that try to interfere with the journey. The journey, according to the *Qabalah*, is headed toward the state of *keter*—the celestial throne, "where the glory dwelleth." At times we stray, we go beyond our path, we become enmeshed with our non-intended souls, but then with perseverance we reach the One who helps us open the gates leading to places where the next step in our journey may occur.

Racheil mevakah al baneiha

Rachel bemoans her children's fate (Jeremiah 31:14).

So spoke Jeremiah. He thought of Rachel, Jacob's wife, who never returned to Jacob's home, never met her aunt (and mother-in-law), Rebecca, or her uncle (and father-in-law), Isaac. Yet her soul lived on, and she concerned herself with her descendants' fate.

We Jews believe life never ends. Parts of us die, or cease to live, while other parts continue forever. The *Zohar* says that each soul has 36,000 reincarnations before rejoining the primal soul of the universe. We are forever protected. The mothers of yesteryear have in their soul a capacity and an inclination to concern themselves about us, their future children, about our fate and destiny.

How is this concern manifested? First is the realm of faith. When we say, "In Your hands I entrust my spirit and body. When I am asleep and when I am awake, *Adonai* is with me. I am not afraid," we're invoking and energizing the spirit that watches over us, *Adonai.* But Jeremiah says that spirit has helpers. Rachel is one of them. Jacob had helpers, too—he saw them in his dream, ascending and descending. He knew it when he said, "if you will be with me then I'll tithe all I own." They protected him through thick and thin, and his beloved wife, says Jeremiah, continued in that vein, became the protectress of their descendants. How? By crying out, *mevakah,* and knowing the tear-drenched prayer reached its destined recipient, *Adonai.*

God Bless America

Why do the nations conspire, and the peoples plot in vain?
The kings of the earth set themselves, and the rulers take counsel
together, against the LORD and his anointed, saying, "Let us burst
their bonds asunder, and cast their cords from us."
He who sits in the heavens laughs; the LORD has them in derision.
Then he will speak to them in his wrath, and terrify them in his fury,
saying, "I have set my king on Zion, my holy hill" (Psalms 2:1-6).

Why do the nations unite and conspire without success?

Nations—many of which are not democracies—bond together and criticize God and his servant, the leader of the free world, saying: "We do not want our economy to depend on you!"

But the president and his counselors laugh; God makes sure the united nations are not able to agree on any single resolution to condemn his policies. And in the near future, God will speak to them in his wrath, he will terrorize these countries in his fury, saying, "I put the President in the White House, I made him the ruler of Capitol Hill!"   *DJT*

Ve-yivtichu be-kha yodei shmekha

Those who are aware of Your true name place their trust in You (Psalms 9:11).

At the naming ceremonies of our children, we ask parents to tell us why they have given their newborn child this name and not another. Oftentimes, the name is chosen to continue the connection to a person who has deeply affected us. In doing so, we hope the honoree's energy will be inherited by the newly named one.

Our tradition teaches that a name, besides identifying a person, is also a commentary on his or her life, past, present, and future. It tells us in a concise way what he or she is now and what he or she may become. Thus the true knowledge of the name clarifies the life yet to be of the bearer of the name.

In the Jewish mystical tradition, many formulas were arrived at, hoping thus to fathom every word's meaning, every name's energy. Among them was a form of numerology called *gematria*. My Hebrew name is *Tzvi*. The $Tz = 90$, the $v = 2$, the i or $y = 10$, the sum is 102, which when the digits are added up, totals three. Three is a sacred number; therefore, over the years, I assumed my purpose in life was a power of the sacred. We also have the verse, *tzadiq* (the righteous one, the God-associated person) *be-emunato* (by his faith) *yichiyeh* (continue to life). It seemed almost as if it had been my life's task to live not the life of ego, the world with all of its ups and downs, but to live my life by whatever eternal message was given to me by the God-spark within me.

A name is more than a hook upon which to hang your hat; it is an announcement telling who you are and what you may yet be.

U-ve-maqhalot rivavot amkha beit Yisrael

Your people Israel consist of many communities
(from Pesuqei de-Zimra, *traditional Shabbat liturgy).*

The second paragraph of the Shabbat liturgy begins with the above phrase. "Your people Israel consist of many communities (*maqhalot rivavot*). They're not like other communities. No one can point to anything specific and say, "This is the final version of Jewish law and lore." It's always changing, it's always evolving and assuming new forms and new traditions. In some congregations on Saturday morning, you have as many as seven different services, each stressing another aspect of Jewish experience. It's called the "alternative" way. In fact, our Sages teach us that the *Shema*, our most sacred prayer, can be recited in any human dialect or language. If, for instance, you are completely unfamiliar with Hebrew, and you decide to recite the *Shema* in your native tongue, God would accept it. If there is such a thing as Jewish heresy, it's the notion that whatever is new is forbidden by the Torah. You might ask, "If such diversity is legitimate, what can we point to and say, 'This is the core of Jewish belief?'" Maimonides tried to give us a set of beliefs that he called the *Ani Maamin* (I believe). Edmund Fleg has a wonderful statement: "I am a Jew." It captures in modern terms what some would call the essence of Jewish belief and practice. There have been others:

The Orthodox movement, the Conversative movement, the Reform movement, the Reconstructionist movement, etc. In my eyes, it seems, our belief and practice is of our own personal choosing. After all, the text tells me that God placed something of Himself in me or in the first human, and it's that something which identifies me as a living being. I therefore feel I must tune in to that something to find what my tradition means to me.

Bismi Allah al-rachman al-rachim: Araayta
alethi yukathibu bal-deen?
Fathaika alethi yaduu al-yatima wa-la yachuddu
ala taahma al-miskieeni (Arabic).

In the name of God, the most gracious and most merciful: Do you know
who really rejects the faith? That is the one who mistreats the orphans
and does not advocate the feeding of the poor
(Quran Al-Karim, Sura 107:1-3).

Unfortunately, in our divided world, we often lose sight of
the universal gems that emanate from many spiritual circles.
The above-quoted passage from the Quran can also be
found, in perhaps different words, in Christian and Jewish
sources. The prophets of the Hebrew Bible constantly be-
moan the fact that there were people sitting on marble
couches in Samaria, oblivious to the suffering of the poor
masses around them. We all know the story of Mother
Theresa, her noble life, her living among the poor of Calcutta.
Wouldn't it be an act of supreme *tzedeq* to gather together
these various passages and let them become our new universal Bible? If we could discover the universal good in all of us,
then the warmongers, the hate-spewers, the destroyers of the
fabric of human life would be stilled, and their words would
become the hollow echoes they deserve to be.

Every one of us has experienced a moment when "A gen-
tle word allays wrath, a harsh word provokes anger" (Prov.
15:1) and "A patient man calms strife" (v. 18). Never give up.
Never say to yourself, "There's no hope." Never assume that

whatever you've done is final and can never be redeemed. This is the essence of our faith.

If only we could adopt a new way of living and be constantly open to change and to new traditions, how different life would be. If we are determined to quote the past, let's find the positive and lay the negative to rest.

Va-yomer Adonai salachti ki-devarekha

And the Lord said, "I have forgiven according to your word" (Numbers 14:20).

Our detractors have insisted many times that Judaism is a religion of law, while its sister religion, Christianity, is one of compassion. I've always wondered why. How do people arrive at such conclusions? Having been raised in the bosom of Judaism, having watched the responses of our people to dire and taxing moments, having witnessed acts of compassion and outreach, I ask, "How can you say that about Judaism?"

My proof-text is the above statement: *va-yomer Adonai salachti ki-devarekha*. Moses speaks to God, complains about His harsh judgments, and God says to him, "I will forgive, as you have suggested." From what we know of autocrats and authoritarian figures, they will seldom say, "You're right." The opposite is true. Remember the story of the Queen of Hearts? When someone disagreed with her, she immediately shouted, "Off with their heads!" Our God isn't that way. He says, "You're right. I've changed my mind. They are forgiven."

I would carry this statement a bit further. I think this is the inkling of depth psychology. What do depth psychologists tell us? That the ultimate that is the soul within us is our God-spark, and that spark does not judge the way we humans do. It's very sympathetic. Even though you've taken a course of action other than what society might ask for, you are still not to be condemned. If anything, you are to be applauded, for you have found what your soul is asking you to do.

Don't Let the Facts Ruin a Good Story

*When Herod died, an angel of the Lord suddenly appeared
in a dream to Joseph in Egypt and said,
"Get up, take the child and his mother, and go to the land of Israel, for
those who were seeking the child's life are dead."
Then Joseph got up, took the child and his mother, and went to the land
of Israel. There he made his home in a town called Nazareth, so that
what had been spoken through the prophets might be fulfilled,
"He will be called a Nazorean" (Matthew 2:19-21.23).*

The biblical narrator, here using the voice of Matthew the tax
collector, answers the vexing question of early followers of
Jesus Christ: How could someone from Nazareth be the
Messiah? How could he be related to the house of David?
Matthew explains to us how Jesus' family originally lived in
Bethlehem, Joseph being a direct descendent of the great
King of Israel, just as it was predicted in the Scriptures. And
his parents move to Nazareth fulfilling what the prophets had
spoken.

However, nowhere do the Jewish Scriptures refer to Nazareth, the town is not mentioned in the Old Testament.
DJT

Al tipol adam eimah yiteirah betokh beito

A man should not bring extra dread into his home (Talmud Gitin 6b).

The rabbis of old, the Sages quoted in the Mishnah and later in the Gemara, showed their insights about life and nature. At their regular sessions, stories were told, anecdotes pertaining to every phase of life was on their agendas.

One of their maxims is quoted above. One should never bring home exaggerated fear, anger, or any other extreme emotional energy. The idea is quite modern. Once you leave your workplace, or any other place away from home, don't bring with you the tensions of the other place. Some of us would say, "One can't compartmentalize." Emotions aren't mere faucets to be turned on and off at will. If anything, we know our emotions, if not resolved, can become festering sores within us. These sores tend to hide behind other surfaces. They may affect our immune system, our digestive tract, or other parts of our bodies. These sores can become the energy that stirs up our negative, destructive behavior. Many times, the exaggerated fears and frustrations are due to the conflicts of the workplace. When brought home, they often disturb the quiet atmosphere of one's life.

*Anokhi anokhi hu menachemchem,
mi at va-tiri me-enosh yamut
u-me-ben adam chatzir yinaten?*

*I alone am He who comforts you,
what ails you that you fear man who must die,
mortals who fail like grass (Isaiah 51:12)?*

I've been asked many times to explain the sorrows of this world, the pain and suffering so many of us go through. I've had to do this in my own life, yet somehow I have come to the conclusion that all of life is interconnected, all of nature is part of single scheme. All of the secrets buried beneath the deep surface are waiting to be discovered. God has given us the power to be the great investigators. God doesn't say to us, "Here you may tread, and there it is taboo." All of nature is the human playground. So therefore it ill behooves us, at any time in our life, to say, "The *only one* who can help me at these crucial moments of life, when questions stare me in the face, is another human." Isaiah says it clearly: "I alone am He who comforts you, what ails you that you fear man who must die, mortals who fail like grass?"

Go beyond the ephemeral. Don't rely on princes, says the Psalmist, on individuals who can't help you, but rather place your trust in *Adonai*. He is the one who can help. He is the shield that can protect.

I am sure that some of you reading these words or perhaps hearing them will say to me, "This is too simplistic." Why must the great answers always be profound? It's in the small voice, in the obvious moment, it's in the solution that stares you in the face in which many answers will be found.

To Point to the Bird

Look at the birds of the air; they neither sow nor reap nor gather into barns, and yet your heavenly Father feeds them. Are you not of more value than they? (Matthew 6:26)

When a German driver signals dissatisfaction with another driver, he or she may point their index finger to their head. The gesture is called *den Vogel zeigen*, to point to the bird. It is very impolite, and I do not suggest you try the gesture in public. The expression reflects the word of Jesus according to Matthew. When it came to talking about existential worries like food, clothes, housing, or finances, Jesus simply "pointed to the bird." *DJT*

Ve-el mi ke-damyun El,
o-mah damut kalchulo

To whom can you then liken God?
What form compares to him
(Isaiah 40:18)?

The third of the Ten Commandments states, "Thou shalt not make for yourself a sculpted image or any likeness of what is in heaven above or the earth below. You shall not bow down to them or serve them." Traditionally, this has been interpreted as an admonition not to worship idols. Let's look at the text carefully. It is saying, don't take any part of nature and call it God. That's what Isaiah meant. To whom will you compare God? Why are you wasting time and energy in assuming that a part of God's created world is God in toto?

This doesn't point to instances when humans say to themselves, "My God, I am so infused with your spirit, I wish I could represent it so people know what I am talking about." If you draw a picture, or paint a painting, that isn't idolatry but rather a moment of exaltation, when you are thinking "I've got to say something, it overwhelms me."

In the seventeenth century, Jewish mystics, people of the spirit, and others would walk through the streets and say, "Wherever I turn, God is there. East, west, north, south, there God is." If I look at a budding tree, I'm reminded of God; if I see a little bird, I'm reminded of God; if I see a fish, I'm reminded of God. And since we don't want to confine God, we say, "God is *Adonai*, the one whose name cannot even be uttered or pronounced, whose limits are beyond infinity."

Ve-lo diber Adonai limchot et shem Yisrael mi-tachat ha-shamayim

And the Lord resolved not to blot out the name of Israel from under Heaven (II Kings 14:27).

We of the Jewish faith have always had to contend with our minority status, though we shouldn't be surprised since the Book of Deuteronomy says, "You will be few among many; that is your destiny." What does that mean, "You are few among many?" First, it teaches us that no matter what we may be facing, no matter how devastating it might be, no matter how final it seems to be, being few among many means you will never be decimated. We know, even those places where in previous generations we were expelled, somehow a way was found to return. Even though millions were consumed during the Second World War, somehow some survived and because of them there are again flourishing communities. For it is our deepest belief, as we've stated above, "The Lord resolved not to blot out the name of Israel from under Heaven."

This is a working premise for us. No matter what may happen, a remnant will always endure. In wider terms, we Jews have never said that this is only a blessing for Jews. We have found many people throughout history who somehow found wisdom in our texts, and said, "May I please circulate among you? I don't intend to convert or wipe out my past, but I want to drink from the font that is yours." Many among us said, "Welcome. Sit down at the table," for the promise of Adonai to us, we feel, is a promise made to humankind.

Va-yavo ha-melekh David va-yeshev lifnei Adonai
va-yomer mi anokhi Adonai Elohim
u-mi veiti ki haviotani ad halom

And King David arrived and felt he was in the presence of Adonai,
and he said "Who am I? Adonai, the Great Judge.
And what is my family or kingdom, that you have brought me to this
place?" (II Samuel 7:18).

We who have been raised in the Western world have been told time and again to be humble. To be humble as Dickens would portray it is to subsume your very personality, your very essence, to the point where it is not longer in the picture. The Jewish way, as expressed in the Hebrew Bible, approaches life differently, as if to say, "It's no great blessing to make yourself into nothing; it is expected of you that you present yourself as you really are. Let your yes be yes and your no be no, the Sages teach us. Don't play pious games. Don't think that by abnegating yourself you are displaying strength; it's not so. God gave you a mind, he gave you a heart, and he gave you your own set of nerves, and he says to you, "I gave them to you, use them, don't mute them." It's true that at times you have to bridle all of your temptations and desires. Instead of wiping them off the map, though, address them so that they become your allies in your life adventure.

Bereshit bara Elohim et ha-shamayim
ve-et ha-aretz

In the beginning God created Heaven and Earth (Genesis 1:1).

The Torah begins with the phrase *Bereshit bara Elohim et ha-shamayim ve-et ha-aretz* (Genesis 1:1). This has been translated in many different ways. The common translation is, "In the beginning, God created Heaven and Earth." But when we question this, other interpretations seem to arise. If you follow the construct of the Hebrew sentence, especially the first Hebrew word, *Bereshit,* things catch your eye. First, *Be-* can mean "with" or "when." Using the first word, we can say, "with *reshit*" *Elohim* (God) created Heaven and Earth. What is *reshit?* According to the *midrash, reshit* is another word for Torah, thus, the translation would be "By consulting the Torah, God created Heaven and Earth." The implication is that the Torah pre-existed the world. The Torah, later mentioned in Exodus as having been given at Sinai, might or might not be the same Torah we're talking about. Like many ideas in Jewish thought and tradition, this has to be placed in the category of *teku.* At the End of Days, when Elijah will reappear and announce the imminent coming of Mashiach, we'll find the answer. In the meantime, be satisfied with the various interpretations being presented. Let's look at a second interpretation: *be-reshit* would mean, when at first God created Heaven and Earth. The question arises, "How do we know what 'at first' is?" After all, we are speaking of a period prior to creation, so what system of time existed before then? This leads to another assumption. Some interpreters take the Hebrew word *be-reshit*, put aside the *be-*, take the consonants, *R-Sh-T* and say "This is a *reshet* (a web)." Therefore, the translation would become "With a web, God created Heaven and Earth." Thus like a spider, he spun a web that contained what was necessary and abandoned whatever else was floating around. So to all of us, the study of texts can be greater than any mystery story. And as the comic would say, "you takes your pick."

In trying to deduce the meaning of the first Hebrew verb in the first sentence of the biblical text, *bara*, consider the teachings of the mystics. Much can be found in the word *bara*. First, in *gematria*, the mystical science of numerology, *bara* equals 203. 203, with digits totaled up, is five, which leads some to say, "In the beginning, God had in his possession the first five books of the Bible." The word *Torah* itself, in *gematria*, is 605, totaling 11, which broken down further, is 2, implying that *Torah* is a reality when it's in a dialog, between two. Torah should never be studied by oneself. In the *Ethics of the Fathers*, we are told "When two people are together, God is there with them." In other words, Torah can only be completely understood in a dialogical situation. One should always seek a partner when studying Torah, don't try to study by yourself. Therefore, when God tried to create the universe, he too had to go into a dialog, and the partner in that dialog was the Torah itself. The word Torah stems from the Hebrew verb *yaro*, which in gematria is 215, which breaks down to eight, which describes a double quaternity. Most mystics claim that the most perfect structure is the square, the quaternity, and interpreting the verb *torah* to equal eight, meaning a double quaternity, a special wisdom is noted.

Yom irah ani eleikha eftach

On the fearful day, I will trust in You (Psalms 56:4).

How shall we confront fear? When fear overwhelms us and interferes with our daily functions, what should we do? Some say, "Stand back" or "Take a deep breath" as if that will cause the fear to dissipate. Some say, "Pray for guidance." What if your prayers are ignored or worse, are never received? Others say, "Fear, like other emotions, stems from a deep place in ourselves, so it is incumbent upon us to either confront it or to address it." How much easier said than done!

The Hebrew word in the above phrase, which we translate as "fear" is the same verb we translate in other instances as "respect or awe." If I'm in a state of unknowing, of not being sure of the moment, then one course is open to me: to rely on or to trust You, *Adonai*, My God. The Psalmist is instructing us that when you are in a state of not knowing how to act, where to turn, you are unsure about the future, then say to God, "I'm in the state, and I put my trust in You, for You are the one in whom all gathers and resides." The not-knowing becomes an arena of trust. I may not know what to do, but deep inside of me, I hear the word trust, *B-T-Ch*. In gematria, the sacred science of numbers and numerology, *BTCh*=19, which when the digits are added, is 10. When one is in a state of fear, one has but once choice, *B-T-Ch*, trust. For in a state of trust, only You and *Adonai* exist, and the rest of existence doesn't impinge on you. Fear is gone.

Too Much for A Pig

They came to the other side of the sea, to the country of the Gerasenes.
And when he had stepped out of the boat, immediately a man out of the
tombs with an unclean spirit met him.
Now there on the hillside a great herd of swine was feeding; and the
unclean spirits begged him, "Send us into the swine; let us enter them."
So he gave them permission. And the unclean spirits came out and
entered the swine; and the herd, numbering about two thousand, rushed
down the steep bank into the sea, and were drowned in the sea
(Mark 5:1-2, 11-13).

I took the trip from Gerasa, modern Yerash in Jordan, to the
banks of the Sea of Galilee, about 65 kilometers or 90 minutes in a modern car on very acceptable roads. The Germans
have an expression, when something is simply too much, you
may say, *Das hält ja kein Schwein aus!* "This is too much for a
pig." Mark probably got the name of the city wrong. To run
65 kilometers from Gerasa to the banks of Lake Galilee is too
much for a pig.   *DJT*

Genesis 12

The story of the people later known as the Jewish people begins in Genesis 12. As in many other places in the Torah (the first five books of the Hebrew Bible) we are suddenly presented with *Adonai's* approach, in this case to Abraham. *Lekh Lekha*. It is usually translated as "go forth." Various interpreters translate it differently. The *Mei ha-Shiloach* states "Go forth and find your authentic self. Learn who you are and who you are meant to be." This is the essence of the Jewish spiritual journey. Learn who you are and who you are meant to be, implying you are not destined to be an automaton, living and reliving the past. "Go to yourself. Leave your native land, your birthplace, your father's house, and go where I (God) will lead you, to the place of your own vision." Once you have done that and have become a new beacon, show the way of personal vision, the you who will bear a new message, for ultimately a great nation will evolve. I will bless you so that you will be a blessing for others. "Whoever blesses you I will bless, whoever curses you, or wants to eradicate you, I will destroy." For the beacon you will become will affect all who are near and far and wide. Through you and because of you, all of the families of the Earth will be blessed. From Abram will stem the three acknowledged Western faiths: Judaism, Christianity, and Islam.

One of our deepest Jewish teachings states, *kol yisrael arevin zeh le-zeh*. Every one of us is connected to each other. In days gone by, some have said this only applied to Jews among Jews, but from the days of the Second Temple onward, there was always the concept of friends of God, those who while they may not have taken onto themselves all of the rituals and "sacred acts" of Jewish living, nevertheless, their psychology was that of believers. We think we've reached a point in human history where we must say that all of us humans are responsible for each other, no matter what our particular faith community may be.

I recently received a letter from a local pastor in which he states that the division between Jews and Christians is so great that he can never allow a member of the Jewish faith to participate in Sunday services. To me, this is a step backwards. During the '60s, '70s, '80s, up to the early '90s, I was a welcome preacher in that congregation, sometimes as often as once a month. The purists among us are forgetting that the only truly pure thing is God himself; the rest of us will always be on a journey. We're forever missing our marks, but ever discovering the father who takes back his prodigal child. Are any of us prodigal? Are any of us saintly? Aren't we all one and the other at all times?

Arbaah peamim baqeish Mosheh me-lifnei ha-Qadosh Barukh Hu ve-hashivu im yaaseh shealotav im lav.

Four times Moses asked God to answer him, "Will you grant my requests or not?" (Rashi's commentary on Numbers 12:13)

Even Moses felt the need at times to go beyond blind faith. Even Moses felt that God owed him an answer. Even Moses felt that to ask anyone to suspend their sense of belief and faith is a hindrance rather than a help. In Jewish tradition, the word for prayer is *pilel*; it means "conversation." We Jews feel that we are involved in a continual conversation with the One we call our God, and silence is no response.

Abraham Joshua Heschel, in trying to explain God's response to our cries for help during the Holocaust, said, "God withdrew." He was very disturbed, for he too felt like Moses, "I'm entitled to an answer." In our sophistication, we've learned that God responds in many ways, sometimes directly, sometimes by innuendo, sometimes by opening our eyes to what lies before us. In all cases, there is a response. A young child once approached her father and said, "I pray every night, but I don't get any answers." She withdrew, returned a few minutes later, and said, "God answered. He said 'No.' " Out of the mouths of babes, wisdom sometimes comes forth. God answers in many ways.

We have to practice the art of discovering the answers. Some tell us that, in quietude, the answers appear. Others tell us that in unexpected moments, we find answers. I personally feel that the answers follow a trajectory of their own and will appear when the trajectory brings them to point of appearance.

We are taught, *kol ha-merachem al ha-briyot me-rachmin alav min ha-shamayim.* When we show compassion for another human, a plant, an animal, a fish, or a fowl, we are rewarded with compassion from heaven, from God, from nature itself. Compassion ignites compassionate. Love ties one to another. When Scripture tells us, "You shall love *Adonai* your God (or your neighbor) like yourself" the verb used is *ahav. Ahav,* usually translated as "love," has a secondary meaning, namely "linkage." When you experience the sensation of *ahav,* you are experiencing a sense of linkage to the object of your *ahavah.* Thus, the highest level of any relationship becomes *ahav.*

When I am in love with someone, I'm oftentimes blinded. I don't see the cracks, the fissures, the negatives in that person's life. Thus, the text is trying to tell us to try and reach a state in which you can see yourself relating to God or to a person and say to yourself, "No matter what, in my eyes, all that I can hope for has arrived."

It may seem to you as though the impossible is being asked for here. But think a moment: Isn't it true that once you find yourself on a plane of completeness, of oneness, you are also on the plane of surrender? "I don't care," I say to myself. "As far as I'm concerned, nothing will ever match the love I have with my love-object.

Our sages teach, *Ein somekhin al ha-nes*—"One must not become too dependent on signs, portents, and miraculous moments" (Talmud Pesachim 64b). The word *nes* is usually translated as "miracle." If truth be told, it really means "sign." Don't spend your life howling and screaming, "Show me a sign!" Signs don't come from nowhere. We of the biblical tradition have always said, "As you sow, so shall you reap."

You want a sign? Do some planting. Don't just sit back and say, "Show me a sign!" It won't happen. That's not God's way. Even when God extends to us a moment of grace, the desire for it has to be communicated by us. God responds to the one who calls.

How does one communicate with God? Some say, in the stillness of the night, in the stillness of your soul, in the stillness of nature's beauty. If you follow any of these three courses we've just mentioned to you, you are engaging in an act of connectedness. There is no closer path to God than an act of connectedness, of being one with any part of God's creation, whether it be the trees, the birds, the fish, or the humans. God is not a fragmented piece of life; God is the totality, the one from whom all that is life emanated, and the one to whom it is always redirected. The more connected we are, the closer we are to God. In Jewish tradition, it's been taught: *devarim ha-yotzim min ha-lev nikhnasim el ha-lev.* That which comes from the heart (core, essence) of one will find another heart with whom it will connect. The same is true for God.

We can imagine the anxiety of the author of this Psalm. Up to this moment, he felt God's presence, but something happened: the presence withdrew, and he became confused. The lesson conveyed to us is simple: when God's presence is felt, we feel as if we have a fortress of our own. We have the strength we need, the hope we seek, the compassion we look for, it's all guaranteed. From the author of the Psalm, it would seem that there is no planned program to guarantee such results. It's a matter of faith and belief. God, when called upon, responds.

If you are aware of your own human journey, we are sure you can recall such moments. The loneliness, the sense of abandonment, and the turnaround. We would suggest three steps in overcoming the chasm of loneliness: 1) Sit quietly, and focus on the loneliness, its nature, its cause, and your own personal contribution to it; 2) Place yourself in a different mindset, and recall those moments when you felt as if you were in the fortress of faith; and 3) Say to yourself, "It can happen again." Believe it and live that way.

Qarov Adonai le-khol qorav
le-khol asher yiqrauhu be-emet

Adonai is near to all who call upon Him.
He only asks it be done with truth (Psalms 145:18).

Adonai is as close to us as the air we breathe. Our tradition teaches that *Adonai* is as close to us as the call we make when we seek Him. How close is that? As close as a thread, as close as a whisper, as close as a moment of truth. If I call to Him, it is a true call, one that comes from me. Even if it is not necessarily prompted by what is happening to me, He still responds. Of course, the Psalmist was willing to go further by saying He is as near as the space in which we find ourselves. That's why one of the names by which we know this force, this energy, this being we call God is *Ha-Maqom*, the place, the space where we find ourselves. God is always present. When we are prescient, or consistent, in our attempt to be in *Ha-Maqom's* presence, He is there. Approach Him in truth, not because of current needs and circumstances, but in truth, for that is the way. The truth of which we speak is just that, no ands, ifs, or buts attached. It is God. It is *Ha-Maqom*. It is you and I in our being, the breath that is God is in us, it's the one who responds.

Elohim al dami lakh al tirchash ve al tishqot El

God, please don't be silent, don't be speechless, don't be aloof (Psalms 83:2).

Whatever happens, God, don't play the silent relative. What a fascinating statement! As we regard history and review it, we can hear the falling victims of war, the survivors of catastrophes, the sufferers of plagues crying out *Eli, eli lama azavtani?* Why have you left us? We need you. We can't live without you. You're our fortress, you're the one who can redeem us, and you're the one who can save us. You know this to be true, and when our human counterparts embark on forays, invasions, pre-emptive actions, you know you're not there, because if you were, you'd put a halt to it. It's not your way of taking care of things.

In the early days of June 1967, when we of the Jewish world sat with baited breath, wondering what would happen to the young State of Israel, those who prayed among us cried out these phrases. I recall Abraham Joshua Heschel during an afternoon service (*minchah*), crying out these words: "Please don't be silent again. Don't withdraw."

It seemed to many of us that this time, God responded. Israel wasn't decimated.

Many years ago, I was standing at the bedside of someone who was in a deep coma. Suddenly, he awoke, sat up in his bed, looked over the foot of the bed, and said, "*Malakh ha-maves* (angel of death), leave! You're at the wrong address!" Fortunately, he survived another ten years. There's something to be said for words from the heart, for words of prayer. Prayer in Hebrew is *pilel*, it means "conversation." When I am *mitpalel*, I am conversing with whom I want to reach, and many times I succeed.

One of my favorite verses has always been "Within your hands I entrust my spirit, and my body too. Adonai is with me, I need not fear (Psalms 31:5)." The Hebrew verb for entrust, *paqad* (P-Q-D) is used in many contexts in our sacred scripture. When Sarah gives birth (Genesis 21:2) the verb P-Q-D is used. In this context, P-Q-D refers to extraordinary relationships, beyond the natural or the reasoned. It is a relationship of faith. So when I say, "Within your hands (or within your domain)" I P-Q-D my spirit to him and my body too, I am placing myself in an area of trust beyond question. We know from our human journey that there are times that call for such profound trust. When we're standing at the edge of a precipice and are afraid we may fall, often something tell us "trust" nevertheless. The Torah has a wonderful example of this, when our ancestors stood at the edge of the Sea of Reeds. Moses hears the message "*Adonai* will do battle for you, and you will keep quiet." There are times when we have to place ourselves in a situation that is beyond our ken. We have to reach that point where we can say (although it seems like all will collapse, we nevertheless will say), "Hold on."

Psalms 23

A story is told of a young man who was sent off to school. His father gave him some money to tide him over, but the money didn't last, so he sent his father a letter, saying "Dad, send money." The father was illiterate, so he went to the town scribe and asked him to read the son's letter. The scribe read the words, "Dad, send money." The father's response was, "What kind of son is this, to send me such a letter, 'Dad, send money?' That doesn't sound like my son." He went to a second scribe and had him read the letter. The second scribe caught the feeling of the letter, and in a pleading way, read the three words: "Dad ... send money." The father, on hearing the second reading, said, "Oh. My son is responding to me. I'll send him whatever he wants."

The twenty-third Psalm is a letter sent by a troubled soul to the father, to the Creator. *Adonai* is *my* shepherd, nothing fails me. I don't lack anything, for I know he is with me. He may lead me through the most difficult valleys, but I know in the end he'll bring me to a place of quiet. He'll send me what I need. And the recipient of the letter says, "If there is such close feelings and relationships directly between my child and me, the bridge that exists between us shall never be severed."

Not a Happy End

But he (a young man) said to them (the women at the empty tomb), "Do not be alarmed; you are looking for Jesus of Nazareth, who was crucified. He has been raised; he is not here. Look, there is the place they laid him. But go, tell his disciples and Peter that he is going ahead of you to Galilee; there you will see him, just as he told you."
So they went out and fled from the tomb, for terror and amazement had seized them; and they said nothing to anyone, for they were afraid
(Mark 16:6-8).

These are the last verses of the Gospel According to Mark. In this account the resurrected Jesus does not appear to the women. All they receive is a statement from a young man that Jesus was raised from the dead and they should tell the disciples. But "they said nothing to anyone, for they were afraid."

This sentence is the worst imaginable ending for a gospel, isn't it?   *DJT*

Ha-shamayim mesaprim kevod El u-maaseh yadav magid ha-raqia

The heavens speak of the glory of God;
the firmament tells of His handiwork (Psalms 19:1).

Finding God isn't a difficult task. The Psalmist said, "Wherever you turn, you sense God's presence." Look up and you sense it, look down and you realize it. What are the God-signals in this world? Is there a formula for tuning into them?

Indeed, there are many. Nature itself is a God-signal. Every sensation has its distinctive hue. Autumn colors, spring spray of many shades, the quietude of summer and the white color of winter—all these attest to a power greater than ourselves. Examine the human body, trace its activities, its nervous system, and its chemical composition. It's beyond human creation. Think of the latent power in so many corners of the universe and you can hear your heart saying, "How many are your deeds, O God, O Creator."

Just consider Einstein's theories, his definition of infinity, and his statements pertaining to human brainpower, and you know it is beyond human ken. Surely, a mind greater than the human is involved in creating something so extraordinary. Consider compassion, which consistently seeks expression in the human community, an almost automatic response to human loneliness and isolation. More often than not, we act beyond human social limits when we provide a human touch and encouragement, thus lessening life's loneliness and feelings of abandonment. Who has instilled in us this humane tendency, if not a power greater than ourselves? For logic would suggest "Consider yourself; forget the others. Erect barriers and be suspicious of strangers. Say to yourself, 'You are unlike me, therefore you are an adversary' " But compassion says otherwise. You are in pain, you are of the human family, my heart therefore reaches out to you and my arms extend an embrace. Come let us be one and declare our love for each other!

Amar naval be-libo ein Elohim

The fool says in his heart that there is no God (Psalm 14:1).

As much as we who believe in God affirm this belief, we sometimes find our affirmation is not enough to convince the nonbeliever. We sometimes behave as if the being in the verse "The blessed one spoke and world came into being" is ourselves; because we will it, so shall it be. In many avenues, this is true. But in the avenue of affirming and accepting the presence of God, we can't be the creators. This is a matter of the heart, and each heart has to find its own way to the belief.

The Psalmist says "Those who claim there is no god are *naval* (fools)," as if to say that anyone who takes a few moments, pulls himself away, and just thinks, will come to the conclusion that our existence cannot be explained in any way except by a creator who sustains the world.

Why does the Psalmist insist that one who hasn't realized the existence of God is foolish? He has been through the notion that without the concept of *Elohim*, which is God who set the rules and the foundation of the universe, there would be chaos, the chaos that existed prior to creation. Anyone who insists that there is no order in the chaos is spiting himself or herself. How can anyone continue in this world unless he or she feels somewhere that there is a light at the tunnel's end to take you out of the chaos? In the Talmud, we have the concept of those who say *ein din ve-ein dayan.* There is no code, there's no system, and there's no one else supervising, differentiating between good and evil, right and wrong, dark and light, hope and despair. Remove *Elohim* and you have chaos in its wake.

Much has been written and said about the *nachash* (translated as "serpent") of the ancient Garden of Eden. It is depicted in Mesopotamian art as a four-legged creature with scaly skin. It seems at first glance to be a replica of Ezekiel's creature of four faces and perhaps four bodies.

In Jewish tradition, the serpent, even before the curse placed upon it, was an evil creature, possibly quasi-supernatural (i.e., the dark side of the angelic class). It is sly, it is wily, it is attempting to lessen the power of God's words.

Its first victim is Eve, its second victim is Adam. True, the serpent is punished, but never enough to be rid of it. This has led in depth-psychology circles to see it as an archetype, not only acting and affecting during its lifetime, but also leaving an after-effect unto eternity. The text doesn't say to the culprits, "You are punished forever." It only says, "You've lost your quasi-divine status." You won't live forever, nor will you be become extinct as a species. You will reproduce, but it will not be automatic. There will be pain. There will be suffering. You have now assumed a human form. For you are now conscious, perplexed, and all of the pluses and minuses of consciousness are yours. "The two of them were *arumim* (shrewd), the man and his wife, yet they felt no shame." Now the serpent was the shrewdest of all the wild beasts that the Lord God had made (Gen. 3:1). Thus, the serpent, the man, and his wife were in a separate class, unlike the rest of creation. They were wild beasts, i.e., untamed, lacking consciousness, free to do their own thing.

Earlier we read, "The Lord God told Adam after placing him in the Garden of Eden to till it and to tend it. 'Of every tree of the Garden you are free to eat, but regarding the Tree of Knowledge of Good and Bad, you must not eat of it, lest you die' (2:15-17)." This happened prior to Eve's creation. Once Eve arrived on the scene, she and Adam are described as shrewd beings. They joined the quasi-divine group, associating with the serpent. The serpent engaged Eve in a dialogue. "Tell me about the forbidden tree." "We can't touch it," says she (God never said that to Adam). The serpent proved to her that touching was okay, knowing that she had not heard God's words directly. Like all second-generation stories, she edited it. Neither she nor Adam are condemned forever. They are simply demoted to human states.

What about Cain and Abel, the first Scriptural fratricide story? Two brothers, Cain (*Qayin*) and Abel (*Hevel*). Their birth was a sexual birth, not a miraculous or supernatural birth. "Adam knew (*yada*) his wife (recently named Eve [or *Chavah*]), and she conceived (as humans do) and bore Cain (*Qayin*). He is named *Qayin*, from the verb *Q-N-H*, or *kaniti*—I have gained or acquired. The same verb is used for all contractual arrangements, i.e., Adam and Eve did what humans do, and acquired a child. Unlike other mythologies, it wasn't an act of God, it didn't spring from any part of the body (like Zeus' head) except the natural body space from which offspring emerge. The Lord helped, but didn't bring it about directly. Within a short time, she conceived and bore another child, Abel (*Hevel*). Abel is a keeper of sheep, Cain a tiller of the soil. We have here a description of early settled life. Sheepherders, soil tillers. The question posed was which was higher on the social scale, the herders or the agriculturists? Obviously, the editor didn't side with the latter (the agriculturists), the settled, the gentry (the landowners). For God chose Abel's gift. Here we have the first bias of Scripture. Later, the descendents of the patriarchs (Abraham, Isaac, and Jacob) are told they will never be a settled people. You will always identify with the rootless, the shepherds, the unsettled class and *Qayin's* "punishment" is you too will never be of the settled, so you can share the agony, the frustration, the fear, and the hope for stability that mankind has always sought. The answer, of course, is the breath of God, granted to Adam was never taken from him. This is his eternity. It is in his and humankind's relation to the breath that stability occurs.

In the ancient world, there were cultures that insisted that God dwelled in the high places: mountains, plateaus, Heaven, and elsewhere. It was felt that the sense of distance assured its sacredness. Jewish tradition believed otherwise. It said that God asked us to build him a *mishkan,* a dwelling-place, that He may dwell among us, in the precincts of our lives and our communities. In time, the sanctuary became the forerunner of the synagogue (the sacred place). In many Jewish homes and institutions, the symbolic "dwelling-place" of God is the *mezuzah,* the parchment bearing a case with the name *Shadai* on it (the God Who is forever with us, the Sufficient One).

Another doctrine is that of the *Shekhinah,* the resident, compassionate God Who is forever available to us. These concepts, *Shekhinah, Shadai, mishkan, mezuzah,* are but other steps in drawing our attention to the immanence of God, the God Who is always with us, awaiting our call. From this follows the term *tefilah,* translated "prayer," but truly meaning "conversation," for we are constantly in conversation with Him.

Ancient scholars wondered which concept was authentically divine, and which was man-made. In time, they came to the conclusion that the divine and the human are interconnected and interrelated. In the *midrash* of Vayiqra Rabbah, we have the statement: "God says, 'I have shared with the world a new *torah,* a new way of looking at life. Humans have interpreted it.'" The torah and the interpretation of it have in them the divine stamp. We Jews have never said that God, eternity, and divine messages are suspensions of nature. We've said, in the words of Abraham Joshua Heschel that man is not alone, and man's constant companion is his creator. This is unlike some who said that once God created the universe, he withdrew and let it run by itself. Rather, the Prime Mover never took his "hands" off his creation, never withdrew his energy from it, and never let it run by itself. For some of us humans, this is a difficult concept. We'd like to believe that the whole world is in my hand rather than the whole world is in His hand. The evidence of our existence is always brought to us from our five senses, and we seem to forget that beyond those senses lies a deeper sense which at times we must tap into in order to make sense of what our primary senses give us. What is this thought conveying to us? Three things: 1) Man is not alone; 2) Man is the partner (*shutaf*) of God; and 3) man and God are in a constant relationship, seeing to it that the world survives.

Mi yidmeh lakh u-mi yishaveh lakh u-mi yaarekh lakh

In this, my ninth decade, I am preoccupied with God. Who is God? Who can compare himself to Him? How do you evaluate God, and by what measure do you compare God with other lofty concepts?

Let me begin by saying that I don't believe anyone ever sees God in God's entirety. We get glimpses of Him as Moses did in his day. Yet I at least know He exists. Too many unexpected and never dreamed of things have happened to me for me to doubt God's existence. Let me cite a few: I've met people and experienced events serendipitously, unexpectedly. For example, I've known many people in the course of my lifetime. At times I was puzzled: Why is this or that happening to me? No logical answers were available. Yet, I knew I had to meet them. They said a word or a sentence, and suddenly a light would go on in the darkest part of my mind, and I had the answer to a current puzzle.

After my second wife, Helene, died, I was distraught. I tried to overcome my emptiness by traveling. I went to Europe and to the Carribean within that first year. Yet the emptiness was still there. I was bereft; her daughters didn't relate to me. My children by my first marriage felt a sense of distance. The house I lived in was suddenly a strange place. It somehow wasn't the homestead anymore. Suddenly, then, someone appeared, and little by little, inner doors seemed to open. Long-forgotten feelings surfaced. Unspoken questions were answered. Many responses to my last book, *My Journey*, brought me into contact with types of people I never knew or met before who helped me open my inner doors. I'm sure it was a Power greater than myself. That Power is beyond comparison, measurement, evaluation. It is. That's how I know God exists.

Moani u-meani

Who am I and what am I?

This is a question often posed by sensitive souls. One may say to them, "Look in the mirror, it will help you identify yourself." But does it? Do we ever truly know who and what we are? We must first define the question: If truth be told, we humans are complex individuals. We're in possession of our principal bodies, but there is more. We think, we feel, we react to all encounters. Sometimes our reactions are purely physical: we sense danger and we react; we feel fear and we react; we are joyful and we react. What prompts these reactions? Is it an automatic gesture, or is there something behind the reactions that prompts them to respond? Do we contain our own inner catalog that is attuned to all we encounter and act accordingly? At times, it seems there are resistances within us that restrain us or hold us back. There are resistances that reject the overtures of factors outside ourselves. Persons, things animate and inanimate, that halt us in our footsteps, advances and responses. The reactor can be our spirit, our mind, our soul. One can never know the answers, but one always asks the question: Who am I, and what am I?

Al titchar ba-mireim al tiqane ve-oseh ava

Do not be vexed by wicked people, be not incensed by wrongdoers
(Psalm 37:1).

Freely translated, it means, "Do not be vexed by evil men, do not be incensed by wrongdoers." The power they claim they have is not long-lasting. They may boast, they may speak of legions of followers. Yet, not being bound by any statements of belief or code of behavior, their boasting is like the final plants of the summer season: they wither like grass, and they fade away.

There is something to be said for trusting in a power beyond oneself. There is something to be said for admitting, "I don't have it all; I don't know it all. There are moments when I place my trust in God and in the universe, in something greater than myself." When you do that, you give up anger, you abandon fury, and because of the fact that you are willing to admit your limitations a new strength seems to spill forth from your heart and soul.

"I can't do it all, God. It's beyond me. Open my eyes, show me the way" is not a sign of weakness, but rather it shows you have unfathomable strength. Our world calls for such statements. When we are willing to admit our limitations, then we are ready to reach out to another. When we are suffused with our own "power and strength," we seldom say to another, "Be my brother, let's go together." Life is built on faith, on trust, on unity, on reaching out, and when those things do not occur, then the entire social structure disintegrates.

Ne-um pesha le-rasha be-qerev libo ein pachad Elohim le-neged einav

Sin is the wicked's seer; in the depths of his heart there is no fear of God before his eyes (Psalms 36:2).

The *rasha*, the one who is not an enthusiastic follower of faith traditions, always says to himself, "My source of behavior is not the foolishness of the pious, but rather I am guided by those, like myself, who are convinced that the whole world lies in their hands." He has no sense of the dread of God. He doesn't feel that he's part of the covenant made by God with humans: "I am your God, you are my son." Nor does he feel part of the covenants that are made by the peoples who chose to affirm the existence of *Elohim*. When you have no covenant, no agreement, no point of reference, then you are on your own, and no one can convince you otherwise. So the Psalmist labeled such people *naval,* foolish, drifting, seeing a perfection that really doesn't exist.

One pays a price for this aloneness and separateness. The security that comes with knowing of God's existence and the sense of shelter it brings you can never be duplicated by the one who is outside of this covenant with God. The shelter that is God cannot be measured in physical terms. It's not a tent, it's not a cave; it is a sense of being within a space that is known as God-space.

Family Feud

Jesus was about thirty years old when he began his work. He was the son (as was thought) of Joseph son of Heli, ... son of Nathan, son of David (Luke 3:23, 31).

According to Luke, Jesus was related to King David through the family line of David's son Nathan, whereas according to Matthew, Jesus is related to David through David's other son, the famous King Salomon. Can both lists be correct?   *DJT*

Kol ha-marbeh harei zeh meshubach

He who extends the telling of the story is to be praised (from the Haggadah, liturgy for the Passover Seder).

In the Seder service of Passover (*Pesach*), we find this text. "He who extends the telling of the story is to be praised." The freedom story that is *Pesach* is without end. All our lives, we seek to free ourselves from the chains that seem to prevent us from continuing on our destined journey. We are like the one lost in the forest or in the maze, who can't seem to find his or her way back. Many times it seems as if little hindrances are placed in our way. At times, they seem to multiply and enmesh us. Try as we may, we fail to part this mesh that binds us and escape into a free and welcoming world.

Many times we boast of our achievement, and, within seconds, a reminder appears on the horizon, telling us "You haven't reached nirvana yet." We're tempted to throw up our hands in despair; some even going so far as seeking cures which supposedly can solve everything for us. Our newspapers, our media, and the printed word is filled with panaceas. All of them lose sight of the ultimate message: That freedom is never completely realized, but it is something that must be continually discussed and researched. Therefore, on the Jewish calendar, every seventh day is *Shabbat*, another chance to fathom freedom's lesson. Every *Pesach*, at the beginning of spring, another opportunity presents itself. Don't make the mistake of saying "Aha! The winter is over." It can only be the pleasant and glorious moments of eternal spring. For even spring, if not tended to, can produce brambles, thorns, and thistles, the very objects that prevent the survival of freedom.

Shema beni musar avikha u-torat imekha

Listen, my son, to the tradition of your father and the teachings of your mother (Proverbs 1:8).

This verse captures the worldview of the great teacher we know as Proverbs, or in Hebrew, *Mishlei.* During my undergraduate years at Yeshiva University, a required course was the Proverbs. Dean Saar, of blessed memory, who was a very practical, down-to-earth human, said time and again, "This book will be your most useful companion in life." It's proven to be so for me.

Consider the just-cited verse. "Listen, my child, to the teaching of your father." In biblical tradition, the father, in a well-structured house, was the bearer of the foundational wisdom of the community. This wisdom was called *musar,* ethical, moral, conventional wisdom and behavior. The society was based on the premise that "The less said, the better." Don't judge. Don't hasten to admonish and to scold. In fact, parents were instructed to guide or teach the young person in the child's own way of life, for everyone comes into this world with his or her own inner message, and a wise teacher or guide fathoms it and tries to purify it so that the bearer of the message can find the wholeness he or she seeks in life.

As for our mothers, according to Proverbs, they were the bearers of practical wisdom, called *torah.* This wisdom, once fathomed, opens for you the ultimate path of life. Two and two makes four. The perfect circle and the perfect square.

Mothers are attuned to it, we are told, for the earth itself is called Mother.

Loose Cannon

Say to wisdom, "You are my sister," and call insight your intimate friend, that they may keep you from the loose woman, from the adulteress with her smooth words (Proverbs 7:4-5).

The Greek/Jewish Bible, which became the Old Testament of Early Christians, translates 'loose' as 'from another tribe and evil.' Nothing can be more threatening to a congregation than unattached women. Loose as in loose cannon. She is nowhere at home. Fear of the foreign woman is passed on as wisdom. Between men.   *DJT*

Me-ayin yavo ezri. Ezri me-im Adonai oseh shamayim va-aretz

Where do I find the help I need? I find it in my relation with Adonai, the creator/maker/founder of Heaven and Earth (Psalms 121:1-2).

Ultimately, we want to find the place where we can attach ourselves to nature's main flow. We would rather be part of the stream that is life than constantly try to swim upstream, away from direction of nature's stream. It would seem that many of us find comfort in saying that, somehow, "The rules of life don't apply to me." How often do we cross the street when the red light is blinking? How often do we listen and respond to the great sounds, the thunder, the lightning, the sudden explosions, the extreme political statements, rather than sit back and try to fathom the still, small voice that contains the ultimate message of God.

All of us are in the same boat. It's as if all of us are in an enormous canoe, trying to paddle our way from one shore to another; yet we can't believe what we see and hear, the small, little hints of how to heal ourselves, how to be happy, how to sense wholeness and completeness.

More often than not, we sit back and seek signs, and know that the sign will point to the key, to the winning lottery, the cure that will remove all illness, or possibly the political leader on the white horse who will make everything better. Our Jewish sages told us, *ain somchin al ha-nes*. Don't wish and don't rely on a sign or wonder. Instead accept the old adage, and sit back and wait for the answer that lies within you.

Ve-yavo ha-shalishi ve-yakhria beneihem

Along comes the third and mediates between them
(Baraita of R. Ishmael, Introduction to the Sifre*).*

Our world is becoming a metropolis of divisions. Man versus woman. Jew versus non-Jew (of every ilk and stripe). In the political arena, allies are not sought, but adversaries are constantly created, as if to say *shalom* (harmony) is a dream yet to be fulfilled, rather than a constant reality daily realized.

It seems that the striving voices gain attention. The destroyers, the creators of mayhem and chaos are the heroes. It's as if the ancient battles of the angry beasts and the docile traversers of the earth continues. Can it ever end? Must it always be this way?

It is accepted theory that every part of nature contains libidinous power. In some instances, the libido creates; in others, it destroys. Our Jewish sages teach: "We possess a *yetzer tov,* a good, authentic *(tiv)* nature, and a *yetzer ra,* a destructive, negative nature. The battle for center stage rages between these two tendencies. The turning point comes when the me, the I, asserts itself and chooses its direction in life, for good *(tov)* or for evil *(ra).* At that point, the "I" or the "me," is the third one who builds the bridge over the chasm separating the two.

Ve-yasem lekha shalom. And grant you peace. The phrase "And may he provide you with peace, with harmony, with goodwill," is the final phrase of the *birkat kohanim,* the ancient ministers of the Jerusalem temple. To many of them, the presence of God was as real as the daily breath of air we yearn for. *Shalom* for them was the whisper of this breath. It was akin to the breath infused by the Creator into the first human's pulmonary system, the metaphor being, "Every breath you take can be the harbinger of wholeness and oneness sought by all of us."

For what is *shalom* but the state of oneness and harmony? It's the ultimate gift of the Creator. With it, all is well in our daily world.

When we are in a state of *shalom*, of wholeness, day meets night, sadness meets happiness. When we are in a state of *shalom*, we have reached a moment of genetic wholeness, all of the world, from plant to human is in harmony, drawing their collective breath from the ever-generating energy of the universe. *Shalom, shalom, shalom.*

Mi adameh lakh ... mah ashveh lakh ... mi yirpeh lakh

What shall I attest of you? What is equal to you?
Who shall comfort like you do (Lamentations 2:13)?

One day, Jacob was sitting by his window, perplexed. Out-side, the sun shone, and on the nearby horizon, clouds were gathering. Jacob looked outside and asked, "Who is like you? To whom can you be compared?" He was speaking of God as experienced in nature. The sun is shining, the clouds are amassing. Jacob's experience at that moment was every man's experience. How many times have we ourselves sensed simul-taneously the light of the moment and the creeping darkness that overwhelms it?

We're all light and dark, dark and light, every moment of our lives. We seek balance so that we won't become inflated by our good fortune, nor will we despair because of a trying moment. We strive to find balance in our daily tasks. Can it be done? Yes, if we recall Genesis: "There was evening, there was morning, one day." Night and day, day and night, are the setting of our lives. Neither dominates the scene; both com-pose it.

Be-khol atzmotai tomar na Adonai mi khamokha

With all my bones I shall say, "O God, Who is like You?"
(Psalms 35:10)

Each of us has his or her own definition of God. Some of us refuse to define God, and say, "We know God exists." We feel, in defining God, we are limiting the divine. In doing so, we are not speaking of the ultimate, but of a watered-down version of the God-force. Ask me who God is, and I can't answer you. Any definition I might proffer is limited by my capacity to envision something that is beyond human terms. Why should I worship, respect, adore, sanctify, a blown-up version of me?

The Psalmist solved this dilemma by saying, "I declare *Adonai*, who is like you, with all my bones, with every part of me." One can sense the awesomeness, the *pathos*, of this declaration: "How can I talk about you?"

In the Jewish liturgy recited on Shabbat morning we read: "Even if we possessed the powers of all of nature, its rivers, its wind, its regenerative powers, it would be like a drop of something in the great big sea." One cannot even, in limited ways, express one's beliefs, knowledge, and feelings about God and do justice to one's statements.

Ve-ahavta et Adonai Eloheikha be-khol levavkha uve-khol nef-shekha uve-khol meodekha. "You shall love *Adonai* your God with all of your heart, soul, and might. Is that possible? Can we give our hearts, our soul, our very strength, to one we can never see, but whom we know is there? Can we ever transcend our five senses and believe in the existence of that which is beyond them? Carl Jung was once asked, "Do you believe in God?" He answered, "I know." Thus, there is a realm that we know that is beyond the reach of scientific evidence, yet the question arises, "Is it possible to give our hearts, souls, and power to that realm?"

Some say, "We know." Some say, "Saying 'We know' is the abandonment of rationality." Some say, "We know that, but there is much evidence pointing to areas of life where rationality doesn't reign supreme." There are moments when all of us experience a meta-(beyond) rational moment: when we sense something, such as the power of the wind, the entrancement of the stars. This something operates only in our meta-sense world.

Koh amar Adonai: Tzivaot Elohei Yisrael heitivu darkheikhem u-maalelekhem ve-ashakeinah etkhem ba-maqom ha-zeh

Thus said the Lord of Hosts, the God of Israel, mend your ways and your actions, and I will let you dwell in this place (Jeremiah 7:3).

In previous selections, we've dealt with issues of cause and effect as seen in Jewish thought and theology. Every morning, in traditional synagogues, we recite the passage from Deuteronomy that seems to imply that a nation's respose is dependent on our actions (*ve-hayah im shemoa*). Throughout the Hebrew Bible, we have clauses that begin with *im* (if you do x, such-and-such will occur). In recent years, many have raised questions that show they wonder if life is that tightly connected. What do we leave to chance, and what do we leave to destiny? Some would have us believe that the traditional Jewish approach is so caught up in destiny that there is no room for personal choice.

Some thinkers have pointed out that Judaism is a balance between free will and destiny. It's true, as some said, *ha-kol talui ba-mazal*, everything is dependent on *mazal*, your astral constellation. Others have said, as did Hillel, it's not for you to complete everything, nor can you abstain from it. This delicate balance between destiny and free will and choice is a hallmark of Jewish thinking. You cannot go through the many thousands of pages of Jewish literature and thought and not be impressed at this attempt at balance. Free will means, in Jewish terms, "I thank God for the gift that is me and now it's incumbent upon me to shape it as best I can." In other words, never throw up your hands and say, "I'm stuck. It's all beyond me. I was dealt unfavorable cards." For even rabid determinists will say to you that the game is not in the cards but in the playing of them.

An Evangelical Answer

Philip found Nathanael and said to him,
"We have found him about whom Moses in the law and also the
prophets wrote, Jesus son of Joseph from Nazareth."
Nathanael said to him, "Can anything good come out of Nazareth?"
Philip said to him, "Come and see." (John 1:45-46)

How could someone from Nazareth be considered the Messiah, the Christ? According to John, understanding is not about interpreting the prophets correctly; it is a matter of personal experience. We may not understand God's ways, but we trust what we see, hear, and feel. God is among us! Come and see!   *DJT*

Ve-hayitem li le-am anokhi ehyeh lekhem le-Elohim

You shall be my people and I will be your God (Jeremiah 30:22).

When Jeremiah stated this truth, he didn't list the conditions for this relationship, and he said it in a moment of historical peril. These same words have been repeated again and again throughout Jewish history, for we feel that this covenant of "I am your God and you are my people" is everlasting, never replaced. Throughout our long history, others have come along and said that the covenant no longer applies to us but to them, or that their tradition fulfills the covenant and not ours. In Jewish terms we would say, that's the essence of *chutzpah*. In fact, it's actually the essence of *realpolitik*. The displaced person is never asked, "Do you agree to leave?" He is merely ordered, *aus* (out)! Jeremiah is reminding the world that that's not the way it works. You can't get up on the rooftops and proclaim that you are the new chosen one without checking the more ancient relationships or checking with the God of whom Jeremiah spoke. What says God? Is Jeremiah correct? We say he is. In fact, we never doubted it. We may have strayed a bit and lived in the gray and dark areas of life, but we never gave up. Instead, He is ours and we are His.

A Politician without Values

The words of the Teacher, the son of David, king in Jerusalem. Vanity of vanities, says the Teacher, vanity of vanities! All is vanity (Ecclesiastes 1:1-2).

A political leader insists that our existence follows no preconceived plan, and he is praised. The most powerful man of the nation is painfully aware that there are no values to guide him.   *DJT*

Hineh lo yanum ve-lo yishan shomer Yisrael

The guardian of Israel neither slumbers nor sleeps (Psalms 121:4).

This phrase is repeated time and again whenever Jews gather together. We recite it at burials; we recite it at moments of tragedy; and we recite it when we feel that our faith is being challenged. Any student of history knows that the Jewish experience has not been a linear experience. No matter what formulas we've devised for ourselves, we have no guarantee that they will see us through crisis after crisis. Erstwhile friends seem to be the first to jump on the bandwagon of the mob, of those who say that all that is wrong in this world is due to Jewish plots.

The *Protocols of the Elders of Zion* is the encyclopedia that promotes such thinking. It has been declared by courts of justice to be an outright forgery; yet, again and again, it has been used as the tool of the mainstream of anti-Jewish feeling and belief. What else can we Jews say, except that no matter what these people are saying, that "The keeper of Israel neither slumbers nor sleeps"?

It's true that our tradition tells us that we should not rely on signs and miracles, yet they do continuously appear. Didn't Moses say, "*Adonai* will do battle for you, if you only keep quiet?" Didn't the Maccabees say, "The keeper of Israel neither slumbers nor sleeps?" And didn't our more recent ancestors say, "Never say you are traversing the final road, for there is something beyond your current view, for the guardian of Israel neither slumbers no sleeps.

There is a statement in the Talmud stating that "The fulfillment of a dream depends on the way in which it is interpreted." Every one of us is in a constant state of dreaming. Sometimes we are conscious of our dreams, at other times, they lurk in the back of our minds, trying to gain our attention. In our time and in our society, we are always encouraged to live out our dreams, as if to say, "All you have to do is stick your hand into your vest pocket; you'll find it there, so just live it up."

Dreams are serious business; in fact, I'm convinced that if not for our dreams, we would be in a constantly unbalanced state. Our dreams come to us to guide us, to show us the way out of the mazes in which we find ourselves. No one's life is perfection itself. No one is always blessed with perfect moments, nor is anyone actually cursed with constantly devastating moments. The reason? Our dreams act as a bridge between the reality that we seem to sense, and the inner reality that we can yet achieve. The dream is the signal that calls you to task, that awakens you, that says to you: "Be not afraid. Be not dismayed. For there is a light that is the creative within you." Find it. Embrace it, and even the most devastating moment can turn out to be a bit of heaven.

Lo ira ra

I will fear no evil (Psalm 23:4).

This phrase appears many times in biblical literature. Two examples stand out: 1. "In your hands, I place my spirit when asleep and awake. With my spirit I entrust to You, my body, too. *Adonai* is with me, I am not afraid." 2. "Though I walk in the valley where death's presence is felt, I fear no evil."

This is as if to say, in all circumstances, dire or otherwise, once I place myself in God's power, I know God will take care of me and I needn't fear.

What is God's care, God's power? It entails, first of all, a point of view. I'm not a separate being, unrelated to anything else. God is the symbol for the entire universe, all of creation. In placing myself within the bounds that is God, I am saying I too am part of something greater than myself. Knowing this to be the case, I'm beyond fear, for fear stems from a feeling of aloneness, of abandonment, of no one knowing me or caring about me. Fear is felt when love is absent, for love is the state of being tied to someone other than myself. When in a relationship, and the binds unravel, then aloneness and fear set in. It is the sense of aloneness that leads me to behave in strange ways. In my aloneness, I reach out, I grasp at whatever comes my way, without considering "Is it for me or not?"

There are many forms of the word *qadosh*. *Qadosh* is a central Jewish theme. Many parts of life are designated as *qadosh*. What does it mean? We usually translate *Q-D-Sh* as "holy," or better, as "separate," in a class by itself. Is that its true meaning? Is anything in a class by itself? Isn't all of life interconnected?

Professor Abraham Joshua Heschel taught, "We Jews say: 'Everything has a tinge of *qadosh* to it.' "

Everything is holy by its nature. It loses its holiness when the "holiness" of an object becomes the means or the excuse for destroying another object, person, institution, or program.

If, for instance, I say *X* is not *qadosh*, because it doesn't meet my standards of *qedushah* I have profaned the holy. If I say I have a special bulletin from God assuring me that life lived my way is *qadosh* and lived yours is not—that's an act of desecration.

Qadosh is an all-inclusive concept. The *qedushah* we possess is with us from birth. Each of us is a recipient of the primal breath imbued by the Creator into the first human, and like our DNA, it has been inherited by all humans in generation after generation. Therefore, it ill behooves us to consider the *qedushah* of one to be of a lesser degree than that of another.

La-yehudim hayitah orah ve-simchah

For the Jews, there was light and joy (Esther 8:16).

Every week when *Shabbat* is over, we leave the mystical realm of *Shabbat*. It's special soul. We light a candle, speaking of *havdalah*, the separation of *Shabbat* and its mysteries from the rest of the week, the more mundane existence. The wedding feast is over. It's time to return to the outside world. I've always wondered if it is truly possible to turn off one faucet (*Shabbat*), and turn on another (*chol*). Aren't they intertwined? Can anyone who has tasted the Shabbat experience ever be completely *chol*—completely in this world, oblivious to any other? Can anyone who is solidly rooted in the mundane ever appreciate the sacredness of *Shabbat*? Was Aristotle correct in saying that body and soul are separate entities, like heaven and earth? Or is the other side, the side that says that everything is tinged with holiness, correct? Perhaps we should avoid dichotomies. Perhaps we should see all of life as touched by both the holy and the profane. Perhaps life is a mixture. Therefore, we can seldom speak in terms of purity.

Is purity then a dream, a fantasy? Is the way of God the "absolute" pure way, or is the way of God an amalgamation? Can it be that we are mostly in a dormant state, oblivious to the issues of holy and profane? The awareness of mystical moments awakens us. Thus, the statement at the end, Shabbat to the Sabbath observers.

In this section of our book, we'd like to explore the *aseret ha-dibrot*, the Ten Statements, better known as the Ten Com-

mandments. There are two major points to these ten commandments: one, the affirmation of God's existence, and
two, the affirmation of *lo tachmod*. *Tachmod*, the Hebrew root
being *Ch-M-D*, "yearning," i.e., you shall not yearn for that
which is your friend's, whether it be his wife or his possessions. Can we overcome yearning? Is it possible? Is yearning
to be considered a major transgression?

Supposing I love more than one person. Is that yearning
bordering on adultery? I love my mentor, my parents, my
spouse, my children, my bosom friend, my confidant, my ana-
lyst. Supposing in our love for each other, we explore each
other possibly physically, especially spiritually, on the ball-
field or in close combat. When is the yearning taboo, and
when is yearning expressed for any person other than my
spouse acceptable? Are there God-given boundaries beyond
which it is unacceptable or only human boundaries?

It is important for us, in the present social and political cli-
mate, to rethink traditional premises. Depth psychology has
opened many doors to us. So have our new mores. In Jewish
tradition, we always emphasized two things: first, before legis-
lating or adopting new mores, *puq chaze*, go out into the field
or the marketplace where people are—what do they see as
legitimate norms of behavior? Second, never pass legislation
that people cannot or will not support. The recent to-do
about amending the Constitution is an example of a mis-
guided legislative attempt. St. Paul of Tarsus, who lived a Jewish life, said "The more rules we have, the more sins will be
committed." It's a thought worthy of consideration, especially
for those who, in their zeal for pious living, use the black
brush of condemnation more frequently than the white brush
of forgiveness.

Ve-tiktzar nafsho ba-amal Yisrael

And He could not bear the miseries of Israel (Judges 10:16).

This verse is to be found in the Book of Judges, known as *Sefer Shoftim* in Hebrew. It comes at the end of an incident that presents us with a moment of religious reform. Idols had been put aside; people began to serve *Adonai* again; and, says the narrator (referring to God), "His *nefesh* (soul, spirit) was sympathetic to the miseries of Israel, and He could not bear the miseries of Israel."

In Jewish thought, there is always an interrelation between one part of our body to another, between us and the rest of the world, between us and God, between us and all that we encounter. There is never an untouched moment; rather, there is constant cause and effect. Behind it is the notion that this is the way the world was created; therefore, since we know you cannot suspend nature, miracles as they are usually known in Western thought are really foreign to Judaism. The Hebrew word that is often translated "miracle" is *nes*; however, a *nes* is not a miracle, but rather a sign. It's a guiding light for you that is ready to be captured and interwoven with all that is happening in this world. Thus, no one can ever say, "The Devil made me do it," nor can you spend your life projecting your troubles on another and thus avoid acknowledging them. We Jews believe that when the world is out of kilter, be it the corner where Jews live or one where others live, God suffers a *kotzer nefesh,* the compromising of God's very soul or spirit.

There's a passage in the Talmud that states "the *mitzvot* (positive acts by which we Jews live) were given to us so that we may flourish as human beings." One of the great and early scholars of the Talmud said that God really doesn't need the *mitzvot*; we humans are the ones who need them. It's another gift of God, trying to help us as any good parent would to find a smooth path in life, without obstacles, trials, and tribulations. I personally find a *mitzvah* meaningful to me when I can sit and meditate over it. For in my meditation, I sense vibrations unique to this act. For example, I look forward to *Shabbat* not for the twenty-four hours designated as the day of *Shabbat*, but instead, its spirit. The relaxation I feel on *Shabbat* I don't feel on any other day. Sitting in a chair on *Shabbat* removes layers and layers of tension; a nap taken on *Shabbat* is unlike any other taken during the week. The time I spend in Torah study on *Shabbat* is unique, and it elevates me to a level of consciousness that I don't normally achieve. Shaking someone's hand on *Shabbat* and wishing them a *Shabbat Shalom* has a ring to it lacking at other times. My lifelong meditations have taught me that the rabbis saying that on *Shabbat* we possess an additional soul is profoundly correct. The spirit that is *Shabbat* you don't find anywhere else. In fact, the Talmud tells a story of a Roman nobleman who was invited to a rabbi's house for a meal, and he found it very tasty. The rabbi invited him again on *Shabbat*, and the Roman was puzzled; the meal tasted different. "What spice did you add?" the Roman wondered. "None," was the rabbi's reply. "The *Shabbat* is the spice." So therefore, we can understand the saying with which we began this piece: the *mitzvot* are given to us so that we may flourish as human beings. Again, we have to say to God, "Bravo. You knew what you were doing."

The Rabbis teach: "From the moment that the fetus begins to take on human form, the direction of the life it will lead when it is separate from its mother is being decided." They weren't referring to destiny, but rather to what they considered to be the fact of life. In other words, no one comes into this life as a blank slate, as a *tabula rasa,* but rather as an imprinted text. If this be true, we are who we are almost from the moment of conception: we are the containers of eternal truth. My mother nurtured me, and her nurturance became my life choices.

What, then, happens to free will? If it's all determined from the beginning, what's my contribution as a living being? The rabbis answered: *ha-kol be-dei shamayim chutz mi-yirat shamayim.* At birth, you're a given product, but you also have the free will that helps you choose how you will use it and helps you decide how you will accept that given product. Will you be envious and say you wish you were someone else? Or will you say, "I thank you, God, for who I am?" This has been the dilemma of every human in every generation. One may ask, why do we fight our destiny, or better still, our given Gods selves? Why can't we say "hurrah" for who we are? Why must we always compare and be guilty of desecrating the tenth commandment, or better still, the tenth statement, of Exodus 20. Why must we covet? Why can't we say, "Thanks for the gift that is me?"

I've asked myself many times, "How shall I read a verse of Scripture?" One answer is to be found in the rabbinic literature: "When reading a verse of Scripture, one must place it in context: what preceded it and what follows." In fact, I'm convinced that whole passages of Scripture must be read that way, for there is no linear order in Scripture. The Rabbis teach: *ain muqdam umeuchar be-torah,* there is no chronology in Scripture; this is to say, the author of any scriptural text is presenting us with an idea unique for that moment. Therefore many of the verses that seem to be used in many political agendas these days could be better understood if one approached it as the rabbis did, what preceded and what follows.

For example, in the books of Leviticus and Numbers, we find whole segments unrelated to what precedes or what follows. Many modern scholars have come to the conclusion that some of these passages are ideas so commonly known during biblical times that the biblical author, while assembling the texts, said, "This fits with what we are trying to say. Let's quote it." This is an old literary pattern. The rabbis are concerned that, oftentimes when texts are misquoted, they are misunderstood. Therefore, they say, when quoting a text, one must always quote it *be-shem amro,* in the name of its author. In Jewish tradition, there were moments when the scholars were quite loose in citing their sources: the great Maimonides was faulted by many for not citing sources. To take a verse out of context and not place it in relation to what precedes and what follows it is being untrue to the tenor of Scripture.

We have many texts scattered throughout the rabbinic literature that attempt to arrive at an answer to a question posed at the time of the destruction of the Temple in Jerusalem: why did it happen. It seems that the universal reason accepted by most rabbinic authorities is that the spilling of innocent blood, whether it was by killing or by slandering a human was the cause for the destruction of the Temple as well as the *Shekhinah* (God's presence) vanishing from the Jewish community.

Unlike other cultures, which insist that violence is an heroic sign, Judaism says the spilling of innocent blood is the cause of the downfall of society. Judaism never stresses power and might; in fact, we read in the Prophets, "Not by power, nor by might, but by my spirit, says the Lord." We Jews have felt, from the beginning, that this spirit, this power of God is the lifesaver. Many of our detractors ridicule our lack of blatant, unbridled, irresponsible heroism. Our forefathers didn't measure our success by body counts but by spiritual sparks produced through good and meaningful deeds.

If we grant this premise of the primacy of good deeds and kindness, "by my spirit," then we steer clear of warrior-class and militaristic cadres.

It's been asked: "How can a society support itself under such circumstances? How does it protect itself when threateneed?" Our biblical tradition tells us that there are moments when you just say, "In your hands I place my spirit and my body, too" and leave it to God. Can this qualified pacifism be sustained? We would say yes. Gandhi proved it to be true, and if you listen to what Jeremiah said, he proved it too.

In the *midrashic* collection known as *Tanna de-bei Eliahu Zuta*, we read the following statement: *Kol mi she-sipeq be-yado laasot tzedaqah ve-eina oseh gorem atah le-atzmo*: Whoever has the opportunity to help another (do an act of *tzedaqah*) and doesn't avail himself of that opportunity, places himself in a dangerous state that could ultimately lead to his demise. If an opportunity came your way to help another, and you avoided that opportunity, you have denied your humanity. It's as if you've declared, "I'm not alive anymore." The Sages are so sensitive about one human caring for another that it has become the basis of all they believe. Over the ages, they have been maligned, with many saying that Judaism doesn't know the meaning of mercy. That is the essence of *lashon ha-ra*, and it is a canard of the first order. If anything, the rabbis teach that we are expected to be *rachmanim benei rachmanim*, compassionate people descended from compassionate people.

What is an act of *tzedaqah*? If I see a fledgling bird with a broken wing, pick it up, and nurse it back to health, that is an act of *tzedaqah*. I helped the helpless one. If I'm walking down the street and I see a despondent person, if I stop for a moment and give him or her a cheerful thought, that is an act of *tzedaqah*. If I think to myself, "I have so much, I can't possibly use it all," and I find a way to give my surplus possessions to people who can't make ends meet, that is an essential act of *tzedaqah*. For it to be a true act of *tzedaqah*, we must do it out of the goodness of our hearts, not out of desire for recognition.

Most of us seem to be in a hurry. It reminds me of my children in their younger days, asking me every five minutes, "Are we there yet?" We're never there. We're only in the process of getting there. Thus the lesson should be, don't give in to despair, but look instead for faint glimmers of hope on the dark horizon.

We humans are forever exaggerating our expectations. We haven't learned the first and most important spiritual lesson—patience. To be patient means to be able to say, "Though I may not have what I'm looking for right now, that doesn't mean it won't ever arrive." Nor should we expect what we're looking for to be the exact duplicate of the image our mind produces.

Saint Wolfgang

At the end of two months, she returned to her father, who did with her according to the vow he had made. She had never slept with a man. So there arose an Israelite custom that for four days every year the daughters of Israel would go out to lament the daughter of Jephthah the Gileadite (Judges 11:39-40).

Saint Wolfgang was in need of a church building. He struck a deal with the devil. The devil agreed to build the church in exchange for the first soul that would enter it. When the day came, St. Wolfgang chased a wolf over the threshold. To this day pilgrims visit the church on the shore of beautiful Wolfgangsee in Austria. The devil can be tricked, but Jephtha's daughter had to die. *DJT*

Leviticus 26:3

What's the difference between a *choq* and a *mitzvah*? Some of the classic commentators distinguish between the two by saying that a *choq* is something you do out of faith, a *mitzvah* is something you do out of reason.

Is this really true? Isn't everything really a matter of both faith and reason, walking side-by-side? I believe in God as an act of faith, but my reason tells me that God as defined by Mordecai Kaplan, is the power that makes salvation a reality. How else can I explain an ordinary day that at first seems to be clouded with anxiety and possibly fear, and then, something good happens. Out of the blue, suddenly I sense the fear and anxiety is gone.

What brought about the change? Isn't it possible that the inner mechanism that accepts that God is the power for salvation is activated? Couldn't it be saying, "Silly one. You know in the end that the power will come through, and you are reminded of the Psalmist's statement: 'At night I lie down my pillow is drenched with tears, and in the morning I'm ready to sing again.' "

It's a daily truth

In rabbinic tradition, a cardinal sin is *lashon ha-ra*. By that, they mean the denigration of another, whether in innocence (*be-shogeig*) or premeditation (*"be-meziq"*). *Lashon ha-ra was lashon ha-ra*; there is no excuse for it. In fact, one of the sayings of the rabbis is "Wise people watch their words."

Oftentimes, when reading some of the rabbinic texts, one senses Roman or possibly Latin influence. In Latin there is the notion that a word is like a dagger; once sent, you can't bring it back. I'm sure this thought influences the rabbis too. There is a rabbinic saying that reads as follows: *Kol ha-misaper lashon ha-ra magdil agunot keneged gimel averot: avodah zarah, gilui ha-raayot, u-sfichat ha-damim*—Whosoever indulges in *lashon ha-ra* opens the door to three terrible stages of life (*averot*): first, the worship of idols, because if you engage in *lashon ha-ra,* you are destroying the divine in the victim; then, if you indulge in *lashon ha-ra,* you take a person off his perch and expose him in the worst way possible; and finally, when you ruin a person's reputation, it's as if you have committed murder. Therefore, wise people, watch your mouth!

They especially apply this understanding of human activity to people involved in political life. The rabbis feel that people who seek honor (*kavod*), who would go to any extreme to be noticed, including the denigration of others, are never to be trusted. To them, this is the essence of political office. Thus, the *Ethics of the Fathers* states, "Keep your distance from government officials."

Chanokh le-naar al-pi darko

Teach the child according to its scheme of learning (Lamentations 22:6).

In the old days, we were told "Spare the rod, spoil the child." I'll either beat it out of him, or I'll beat it into him. We look at life differently these days. We realize that a child, from his or her earliest age, has developed its own scheme of learning. We no longer feel that a child who may differ with its older instructor is necessarily a recalcitrant child.

In our school systems, we hear again and again the complaint "My child is bored." Many years ago, my late wife was called to school. Our son, who was a kindergarten student at the time, seemed always to put his head on the desk, completely oblivious to what's going on in the classroom. The teacher was convinced that our son was retarded. My wife came to class, asked the teacher, "What's the problem?" "Look at him," the teacher said. "His head is on the desk! He isn't paying attention." My wife asked, "What are you studying?" "We're doing very important work," said the teacher. "We are studying our colors and numbers." My wife replied, "My son has known this for at least three years. How many years does he have to have a repeat course?" *Teach the child according to his way.*

I've raised this question when I've dealt with the curricula of many schools, including our religious schools. How many times do our children have to study the same set of details of our sacred days? At what point do we teach them the true meaning of the day, rather than the details of them? It's amazing how ready our children are for the deeper lessons.

Eiyekah?

Where are you? (Genesis 3:9)

We're told in the early chapters of Genesis, that when Adam and Eve decided to taste the divine fruits, they felt exposed, and they hid from God's presence. In a very poetic way, the story tells us, God calls out to them, saying, "*Eiyekah?*" Where are you? As if God didn't know! It's a subtle statement. Of course God knows. But humans being humans, sometimes we seem to indulge in things that even God doesn't expect. Our behavior is bizarre, and we're tempted to say, "Your mother or your father never taught you that way," as if tradition and past history are the only factors in human behavior. We humans act, and as a philosopher once said, that's how we know we're alive. We're not placid beings. It's almost as if the editor were trying to tell us that God expected us humans to be like the rest of creation: docile, never picking up our heels, never protesting being "good little beings." Surprise, surprise. We humans aren't that way. Even God has to look for us sometimes.

So what shall we do with the human scene? People like the artist Munch throw up their hands in despair, portraying the human scene as one giant wail of blackness and uncertainty. On the other hand, there have been artists and writers who perhaps realize the reasons for despair but never allow it to become part of the final scene. In Jewish tradition, you have the saying of Rabbi Nachman of Bratslav, "Never consider the road you're on to be the final road. Even in darkness there remains a bit of light remaining to be discovered."

Called to Confuse

Then I heard the voice of the Lord saying,
"Whom shall I send, and who will go for us?"
And I said, "Here am I; send me!"
And he said, "Make the mind of this people dull, and stop their ears,
and shut their eyes, so that they may not look with their eyes,
and listen with their ears, and comprehend with their minds,
and turn, and be healed" (Isaiah 6:8-10).

Isaiah is called to confuse his people, so they will not hear although they have ears, they will not understand, although they are smart, and they will not be healed although there is a cure.   *DJT*

Heve dan kol adam le-khaf zechut

Judge each person with the benefit of the doubt (Mishnah Avot 1:6).

If you really want to understand Judaism, then use as your mantra, *tzedeq tzedeq tirdof,* always pursue the righteous course. How do you do it? How can you be assured that you've embarked on the right road? What if the blackness in another person's life stares you in the face? Should he be immediately condemned, should a posse be sent out, as it was in the old cowboy days, and should he be brought to "justice?" Such justice always ended on the limb of a tree. It was called a "necktie party." Judaism had something else in mind. Before you can decide whether something is just or not, it's incumbent upon you to answer the question, "How did you approach this venture? How did you judge the situation, and what did you say about the culprit?" That extremely insightful collection of maxims known as *Pirqei Avot* (or *Ethics of the Fathers* or better translated, *Chapters of the Sages*) says, "When you're judging someone, be inclined to find a saving aspect in the situation." Don't immediate say to yourself, "Well, it was in the paper, he must be guilty!" or "I heard it on television" or "There was a special bulletin from Washington." Use a skeptical eye, and turn it over, think about it, and meditate over it, before you jump to conclusions. That's what *tzedeq* (righteous) is all about. It's a sober approach to life. It's one that says, "in haste, truth cannot be found." Sobriety asks for quiet moments. You need silence when you read, when you think, when you taste an exceptional morsel, or when you're approaching a situation. So there, take your time, don't be hasty in judgment, and let all the sides of a jewel that is the human be part of the picture.

ve-la-malshinim al tehi tiqvah ve-khol ha-rishah ke-rega toveid

And for the slanderer let there be no hope, and let all evil intentions be thwarted (From the Amidah in traditional liturgy).

And as far as *malshinim* (people who pass stories, true or not), let them be defeated in their purposes, for their end-product (no matter what they say) is evil.

We Jews have always been sensitive to *lashon ha-ra*, the spreading of gossip for good or for bad. The thinking of the rabbis is simple: When you gossip, you are damaging another's soul. You are saying things about someone, and this can lead to a whole train of thought by others ending with personal hurt. In Judaism, ruining one's reputation is comparable to homicide, because if you deprive a person of his or her honor, you are lessening their sense of worth, and thus depriving them of the desire to continue living. That amounts to homicide. No matter how you may apologize for what you've done, a word sent into the atmosphere finds a target and in turn causes great pain and sorrow. All of us are aware of people who were found guilty for some misdemeanor, incarcerated, and then some reporter becomes aware of the injustice, investigates, and finds that the wrong person was unnecessarily accused. His record is still tainted, though, and he seldom is restored to respectability. That's homicide.

Our Jewish tradition has always felt that we are as humans responsible one for another. In fact, in the days of old, any court that sentenced a person to death was considered a court of murderers. One must be extremely careful in what one does or says when another individual is involved.

Mi yidmeh lakh, mi yishveh lakh?

Who can compare to you, and who is equal to you? This thought appears throughout our liturgy. We Jews have never tried to completely define God. We just can't do it. By what standard can we compare God, by what measure can we evaluate God? We know God exists. Abraham Joshua Heschel once said that to him, the existence of God is really the essence of the ineffable. I remember someone in class once said, "But how is that possible, Professor? How can you speak of the ineffable?" His answer: "How can you speak about the possible? Do you ever know anything completely? Aren't you in a constant state of search and research and questioning and requestioning? And when you come to answer, aren't you constantly correcting it, modifying it? The scientist always does this in the laboratory. Why shouldn't we also?"

I think many times as Scripture does. Dreams are sacred. In the dream, many times the answers to our questions appear. Not clearly; we have to dig and dig and dig until we understand them, but they are the answers, we need whether they are questions dealing with our dark side, or with our side of light and faith. Sometimes the images that appear in our dreams embarrass us, and we'd rather not articulate them. But once we sit back and ponder and realize that a voice greater than our own is speaking to us, then the "unacceptable" begins to show its acceptability. It's God at work.

Qol Adonai be-hadar, qol Adonai shover arazim, qol Adonai yechayel ayalot

God's voice is splendor, God's voice shatters cedars, God's voice makes calves skip (Psalm 29:4–6).

The Psalmist tells us that the voice that we call God or *Adonai* is all over, among the *ayalot*, the bleating lambs, in leaves that are falling, in the beauty that surrounds us (*be-hadar*). That which is God is never limited to one thing only. Unlike those who seek fundamentalist answers, we refuse to pinpoint God, for we seek God and we see God at the same time. Ask me, do I believe in God, and I say, "I know." Ask how do I know, I reply "In what I see." Ask me, what are the rules behind my reasoning? And I say there are none. It comes from within me and says "Don't stop. God is to be found all over. There is no place without God." For if you remove God from the equation, you have chaos. Before God stepped in, Genesis tells us, there was chaos. God hovered over the face of the waters (*merachefet al pnei ha-mayam*, Gen 1:3), but only when God stepped in did order and nature evolve.

Seeking and seeing God at the same time also means that we've never completed the journey. I see something but I'm not satisfied so I seek further. A question is answered, another arises. One moment I feel at ease, a few seconds later, the tumult begins again. All of this is part of the God-process. Each of us by our very nature is a seeker. No human is ever completely satisfied with his lot. How often do we say to ourselves, "What's going on here? Why do I feel this way?

What is being said to me? Do I really hear it?" This will be our destiny as long as humanity exists.

Et Iaasot Ladonai

Throughout Jewish history, a clarion call has been "It's time to do God's work" or better still "It is time to do what God demands of us" or better still "asks of us" or better yet "urges us." We never really know what God wants. If anything, the God of today is not necessarily the God of yesterday or of tomorrow. In God's name, as we Jews know it, lies the clue. The name *YHWH* really means "being," and "being" can never be described *en toto*. Being is always in a state of discovery and becoming.

Therefore, the way in which I relate to the ultimate in my life, which I call God, depends on the state I'm in at that time. If I see life in a joyful way and don't notice the clouds but only see the bright hues and colors, then my God is the God of *simchah*, and the urging of the Psalmist "serve God through *simchah*" takes effect. One never knows what the moment will bring, from one second to the next. If I pay close attention, I will realize that my soul is poking around in all sorts of corners, amazed by what it finds.

I am now in my ninth decade of life. Of this I am sure: the God I knew in my first two or three decades is not the God I know now. This doesn't mean I don't believe in God anymore; rather, it is saying that the God of now is other than I knew then. How does God differ for me in these days? First, I am grateful to God for helping me to find the closed doors of my soul and my psyche, leading me to keys that may open those doors, assisting me when I am trying to sort through what I find behind the doors, and helping me integrate the results of my search.

In the treatise *Berakhot*, the first volume of the Talmud, we read: *Kol de-rachmana avid be-tav avid.* Whatever God, or destiny, or anything else that seems to be in control of your life does, it's usually for your good. In their own, quiet way, they are trying to tell you, "Don't walk around with a chip on your shoulder. Admit that there's evil in this world, but don't be overwhelmed by it. Admit that there's a negative side to life, but don't be swallowed up by it. Take a deep breath. Say your own personal prayer or mantra, and move on."

They did not believe that God the creator had evil designs when nature and human creation were concerned. It didn't make sense to them to say, "The one who said, 'It is good' when he regarded his creations would say, in the same breath, 'they are so corrupt; therefore let's wipe them out.'" Nor would they ever say that only a select few have the right to survive because the rabbis believed that *teshuvah*, turning your life around, is an option, and everyone has the possibility of doing it. If they had to choose between *chayav* (guilty) and *zakai* (innocent), they would try their best to follow the latter path. A court that imposes capital punishment once in seventy years is said to be a court of murderers. It is certain that if the *Sanhedrin* were around today, it would oppose capital punishment.

Ki be-simchah tetzeiun

Among Hasidim, these words are sung when greeting the *rebbe*, the erstwhile leader of the sect to which you belong. For the *rebbe* is the symbol of the joy the Hasid seeks. His faith is secure, his spiritual journey leads to higher realms for himself and his followers. Until recent times, the *rabeim* (plural of *rebbe*) were considered to be true intermediaries between man and God. The *rebbe*'s prayers were considered prayers well received by the Almighty himself. Of some it was said the prayer ascended directly to heaven, for they were sent by one whose connection to heaven was entirely secure. Thus, when greeting the *rebbe*, do so with *simchah,* with joy and not despair and fear. Don't be afraid; the *rebbe* will show you the way best suited for your purposes.

The Hasidim were warmed by such ideas. For joy to them was the epitome of human emotion. When one is in a state of *simchah,* of joy, one feels free and at home with the world. *Simchah, S-M-Ch-H,* in *gematria* (the mystical system of numerology) equals 11, the perfect relational meaning. Eleven, the one you adore, you worship is joining you, and together you are joined in the ultimate journey to God's throne and to peace.

I've been asked many times, "Do you believe death is final?" Whoever asks that question has his or her own definition of "final." It can mean the end of any existence. It can mean that what I now know or experience ceases. It can mean the relationship of yesterday, today, and tomorrow has ended.

During my lifetime, I've met individuals who have said to me, "I know I'm living another round of life. My current life dramatically differs from any other I've known."

I recently read of people who have appeared in Jerusalem and, at their hosts Sabbath table, have related Holocaust memories. As if they had lived in another time, another place, and experienced the horrors of the Shoah.

Recently, a woman spoke to me. She taught history in a South Portland high school. The lesson was on Second World War experiences. A handful of local residents raised their hands and said "My parents told me the Holocaust was a figment of some peoples' imagination." She was stunned. No matter what evidence was brought to the class, the students rejected it. "What can I do about it?" she asked me.

I suggested that there are survivors ready to testify. She said they too have been rejected. She came to class armed with artifacts, hoping it would impress them. Again rejection. Finally, one student broke ranks and said, "Even if it didn't happen, the fact that someone could articulate such horror should alert us to the darkness of the human soul." Yes, the voices who continue to speak about human horrors and attempt to reconcile them are dark, indeed.

Ascension

Then he (Jesus) led them out as far as Bethany, and, lifting up his hands, he blessed them. While he was blessing them, he withdrew from them and was carried up into heaven (Luke 24:50-51).

The only other account of Jesus' ascension in the New Testament is given in Luke's Book of Acts. There Luke sets the story not in Bethany but on the Mount of Olives, a few miles away. And whereas Jesus ascends in Luke's Gospel right after he appeared to the disciples on Easter Sunday evening, the event in Acts happens forty days after Easter on a Thursday. No other author in the New Testament has an ascension story. As a matter of fact, Matthew's last line: "I am with you always to the end of the age," reads like the opposite of an ascension. *DJT*

Ashreinu mah tov chelqeinu u-mah yafah yeshurateinu

We are joyful. How good is our lot! How lovely our inheritance!
(From Pesuqei de-Zimra, *morning liturgy)*

Every so often, I'm prompted to take inventory of my possessions, of my health and of my life. When I do so, I come back to the statement in the daily Jewish liturgical service: "How fortunate we are! How goodly is our lot in life, and how satisfying our inheritance!"

I ask myself, Is life really that rosy? After all, in the eighty years of life I've lived, there have been moments full of doubt, wondering about life and life's losses, and wondering about the state of the world. Wondering about the integrity of our leaders, political and otherwise. Yet when I draw back and think not of the outer world, but rather of the inner world that I have inherited, I'm optimistic. I'm sure I can make a case for my Jewish inheritance. Yet when I think of my own bit of history, of the world from which I stem, I'm filled with a sense of good fortune, of "well done."

We've had our heroes and we've had our scoundrels. But above all, we've had our survivors. Some of our ancestors died tragic deaths, suffered terribly for their minority status in many lands. Yet, and this is the essence of the good fortune, books were written about it, ideas were debated and examined. Out of this came new ways of looking at things, seeing scientific evidence not only as proof for the accepted but also for the challenging moment. This holds true for the likes of

Edmond Fleg who wrote in 1927, "I am a Jew," and for Albert Einstein, who gave new credence to God's existence. For the *biluim,* the escapees from Europe who migrated to the lands of ancient Judea and Samaria to make them flower again, who came to America and challenged the status quo, who said that ordinary workers of the sweatshops were deserving of dignity, and that the black neighbor was deserving of social status and mobility. For all this I say, "How fortunate I am," and others too. Life can be good. It need not be the plaything of the selfish and the corrupt.

*

With Adam and Eve's new knowledge, with their becoming conscious of all that human living can provide, they experienced the intimate knowledge of man-woman, birth. The first generation of human living became a reality. It began with hatred, enmity, fratricide. Qayin, the older brother, killed Hevel, the younger one. God chose Hevel's gift to him. Qayin was distressed that his was rejected. God engaged him in conversation, "Why are you distressed? Surely if you do right, there is uplift. If not, sin crouches at the door. It's urge is toward you, yet you can be its master."

In this phrase, "you can be its master," the Torah presents the human dilemma. On the one hand, the human has an instinctual drive (the Torah sees it as the potential for sin, the unbridled drive). It has within itself the power to master it. It is a reminder of the *nachash* (serpent) message to Eve: "God is afraid that once you are at one with your drives, that which leads to good (*tiv* = nature) and evil (*ra* = false friendship, unnatural friendships) are like oil and water. You will be in possession of divine wisdom, and since He isn't sure what course you, the human, will take, ignorance is the better part of valor."

In Qayin's case, all *Adonai* can stress is, "The choice is yours."

In Adam and Eve's case, *Adonai* began by saying, "Don't do it. You will die. You will no longer be the innocent ones."

The *nachash* says, "You won't literally die. You will die to the old way of life to innocence."

God fears the possibility of choice being in your hands. Who knows what you will do with it?

Qayin, after receiving *Adonai's* warning about how sin is crouching at the door (read, "instinct") is always there, invites his brother Hevel to the field and kills him, the first fratricide. What choices did Qayin have? A) To take to heart the lesson of sin crouching at the door and his power to master it, or B) To go with the flow, let the tension of his instinct be his guide.

Torah psychology teaches the need for alertness. Don't give in to your instincts. Master them. In later generations, commentators taught: channel them. Maimonides and others recognized that if not for the *yetzer ha-ra*, instincts, our human nature with its strong sense of curiosity would be abetted and destroyed. Because of it the human would never discover nature's secrets, the very elements that contain within themselves the keys to advancement, to happiness, etc.

In more recent years, we've spoken of libido, the creative urge and its potential for creativity and change, for the discoveries of science and many disciplines. The more conservative among us stand in its way. Their fear of the human (the ancient fear of the Creator) leads us to one-sidedness, some say short-sightedness.

Qayin lured Hevel to the field. The text is abrupt: "And Qayin said to his brother, Hevel ..." What did he say? The Hebrew text doesn't provide any clue. The Greek translation of the Hebrew Bible, the Septuagint, states, "Come, let us go into the field." They went into the field, discussed many issues. Qayin assumed his parents didn't intend to have any more children; therefore, he proposed to Hevel to divide the world between them. Qayin said to Hevel: "You believe in the future. I don't. Let me have this world prior to death, you take it afterwards, since you believe in eternity."

Within a few days, Qayin saw Hevel herding his sheep. He said to him, "The world belongs to me. Why are you herding sheep?" Hevel responded, "I won't abandon them to die." Qayin's ire was aroused, and he killed Hevel. Qayin was then bereft. "What shall I do now?" He knew nothing about the burial of bodies. Two ravens arrived. They had a bitter argument. One raven killed the other and buried it. One version of the story said Qayin buried Hevel, another says Adam and Chavah buried him. All stories say that Qayin tried to get away with it.

Zekhor et yom ha-shabbat le-qadsho

Remember the Sabbath day and keep it holy (Exodus 20:8).

In the early pages of Genesis (or *Bereshit* in Hebrew), we are told that at the end of six stages or days, God the Creator blessed the seventh stage or day, and set it aside from all other days or stages. For on that day, he rested from his labors and took a deep breath (*va-yinafash*). How should we regard the word *va-yinafash*? It's root word is *nefesh*, soul or breath. On the seventh day, God did what he urged the humans to do: take a breath, pull back, review your labor, and quietly sit and say it's good.

In Jewish tradition, *Shabbat* became this weekly celebration. Some who might be living in dire circumstances manage to put aside enough during the week so that on the seventh day, on *Shabbat*, a magnificent meal could be had. It almost reminds you of the legend that says, when God began to create this universe, he gathered together a mound of red clay, and whenever he completed one of his creations, a reminder of it was placed in the red clay. After the end of six stages or six days, God placed within the human a *nefesh* (breath), and the human became a living being. It is that breath that is the assurance of life. The ability to sit back and review your labor and say it's good, the ability to believe that the one who created you is encouraging you to think highly of yourself and go on with the message found in the life that stems from that breath.

Yesh tiqvah ve-toelet

One should never be filled with unquestioning despair. That's a current lesson. The modern physicists from Dr. Paul onward have demonstrated that even in chaos there lies dormant an ongoing principle. Despair and loneliness are not the ultimate answers to the question, "What is life about."

The Bratslaver Rebbe used to say to his students, "Don't despair. *Zert zach nisht m'yaesh.*" Or, as some of his followers sang in the ghettoes of the Third Reich, *al tomar shezo hi darki ha-acharonah*—don't say "this is my final road"—it isn't. The Jewish mystics, great believers in reincarnation, the eternity of matter, the impossibility of ever fully knowing God, the insistence that God is *Ein Sof*, without end, would argue that we are but specks in the enterprise called nature and life.

"Don't despair" is the Jewish message. Don't ever say it's over. It's not. Every moment is but a moment in time and yet it is also a new beginning. It is as if creation is an ever-continuing process. Yesterday's darkness is but the prologue to today's shining light. Don't confuse these statements by calling them naïve optimism. They're not. It's rather potential revealed. Look at your own life. Most likely if you reviewed it with a glass-half-empty attitude, you might be prompted to say, "Why bother? Let's cash in our chips and call it quits." On the other hand, you might say, "Let's conduct a review, an inventory, and see what is worth salvaging and what is worth discarding." It depends on you and your attitude. Do you want to climb mountains or forever remain stationary on a static plane? Choose and carry on is my message.

Part of the rabbinic tradition revolves around the concern with what you are really saying. The rabbis say, "If someone gives his bosom friend many precious gifts while his demeanor is unhappy, it's as if he has not given him anything." Atmospherics play an important part in all of human behavior. Somehow, when we are in another's presence, we can sense his or her mood, and it can throw either a pall or a bright light on the situation. You don't have to say anything. Your face says it all. Thus the rabbis taught us, "Be careful when you say something" or "Make sure, at all times, that no hint of derision enters into your dealings."

A dear friend once said to me, "Don't behave like a scolding pastor, but try and behave like an embracing rabbi." Being open to all vibrations that come my way, I took his words to heart. Every one of us is an ambassador in his or her own right, and no matter what we say, it's not necessarily the words of the moment, but rather a deeper message that comes from within our very souls. You see, we are driven by two forces: One we call ego, a response to world around us, the other we call soul or self, which is a response to all that is within us. A rabbi once said, "We humans can be compared to the marquee of a theater, telling you what's playing inside."

Many of us seem to forget that spiritual maturity is not the possession of only a select few in this world. The rabbis teach that every individual who ultimately comes to a true belief in God, and all those (most often unbeknownst to us) who are at one with God stem from the same stock. The pious are to be found among Jews, among Christians, among Muslims, among Hindus, among Buddhists, and in many other spiritual communities. No one has a monopoly, and no one can claim that God only speaks to the members of their own closed and immediate circle. We have been taught by the Psalmist *La-donai ha-aretz u-mela-o,* the entire universe and whatever within it has the stamp of *Adonai* upon it. It can never be erased. The human quest or struggle is to find it. It's there, waiting to be discovered.

Pious acts don't have to be acts that receive headlines. In fact, piety is sometimes experienced in the most unexpected places. In our community, thank God, there are people who are concerned and who worry about the homeless, the hungry, those who suffer at the hands of others, and try their best to console, to heal, and to bind up their wounds.

Therefore, the saying of the Rabbis, that every individual who ultimately come to a true belief in God, and all those (most often unbeknownst to us) who are at one with God stem from the same stock, is profoundly correct.

The Rabbis teach us that the pious, the examples that we look to in life, are more precious after the end of their lives than during their lives. There's a lot of truth in that statement. We seem to elevate people after they die. We set up monuments for them. Yet somehow, while they are alive we behave as though "A prophet is without honor in his native place." It's like the hungry traveler who comes into an establishment and sees arrayed on the table many delectable foods, but doesn't know where to turn, what to accept and what to reject, for fear that it will have an ill effect on him, rather than abating his hunger.

There is a legend told of *Eliyahu*, the great prophet of Jewish experience and mythology, that he never died and is always among us. He resides in the most humble quarter, ready to bring a divine message to whomever will listen to it. Yet often his message is ignored and sometimes despised.

The same seems to be true of all the spiritual heroes of years gone by, as well as those of today. For example, Martin Luther King, Jr., following his march on Washington, had great difficulty sharing his message with others. Some felt he should be more aggressive and forsake nonviolence, bang a few heads. He refused. He extended his view of nonviolent protest to many areas of American life, and then he was "mowed down." Since his death, he's become an icon, with a special day devoted to his memory and to his cause. The same could be said about the late David Ben-Gurion, Israel's first prime minister, or the saint of India, Mahatma Ghandi, or of Mother Theresa of Calcutta. The list is endless. We've had great people living among us, saintly people, who understood the human condition better than anyone. But driven by nonviolence, they were despised, and weren't considered to be heroes but rather to be fools. Our rabbis tell us it would be a good idea if we could take some of the aura that we afford the righteous after their deaths and give some of it to them during their lifetimes.

The Talmud tells us that if someone intends to do a *mitzvah* and something prevents it, it's considered as if he had done it. *Kavanah* (intent) is always taken into consideration. Not thought alone, but *kavanah*, intent. The Rabbis say *machshavah lav ke-maaseh dami*, the thought is not equivalent to an act, but *kavanah*, that's something else. If someone says to you, "Well, I've thought about it," disregard it. But if someone says "I must do this. I feel compelled to do it," consider it done. What we need in our world is cadres of people with good intentions. From them will come kindness, concern, compassion, and consideration. I may not do it myself, but I'll share my feelings with someone close to me, and that one will be my messenger.

It's so important that we raise our children to be sensitive to their intentions and those of others. How do we measure intent? How do we tell authentic intent from qualified intent? If, for instance, I am aware of the difficulties in my friend's life, and I shrug my shoulders and say, "Isn't that too bad?"

that's not what my friend needs. But if I am aware of my friend's current circumstances, and I try in my own way to help him find another course in life, or encourage my friend in a positive way, then there is true intent. And the same thing is true when I'm about to utter a word of prayer. If I say, "God, I love you" and really mean "I want to be bound to you. I don't want to be a loose cannon, floating around once in a while praising God," then, the energy that is God's will be with me, and my energy that needs directing will be transformed.

Sermon on the Mount

(Matthew 5).

In this section, we would like to consider the Sermon on the Mount (Matthew 5).

In this passage, as elsewhere, we must seek connection to accepted patterns of Jewish behavior and learning:

"And when he sat down, his disciples came to him" (5:1). Dr. Samuel Lachs, in his *Rabbinic Commentary on the New Testament*, cites the first-century practice of studying in the *beit midrash*, the house of study found in Jewish communities. In *The Ethics of the Fathers* we read (3:2) "Rabbi Chananiah ben Tradyon said: 'If two sit together and the words of Torah are spoken between them, the Divine Presence (*Shekhinah*) rests among them.'" The sharing of Torah lessons was commonplace. By the end of the first century C.E., it had become public practice "Our rabbis taught: 'From the days of Moses up to Rabban Gamliel, the Torah was learned only standing. When Rabban Gamliel died, sickness fell upon the world, and they learned the Torah sitting (Talmud Megilah 21a).'" Editorial comment: Could this be the beginning of the plagues, illnesses, sickness, that Jesus seems to have been called upon to cure? The Sermon on the Mount was a public teaching.

"Blessed are the poor in spirit." I am taking the word "blessed" along another track. In the Greek, the original word is *makariai*. It is a direct translation of the Hebrew word *ashrei*, found in Psalms and elsewhere. *Ashrei* is always rendered *makariai* in the Septuagint. *Ashrei* means "happy" or "fortunate." It was a distinguishing feature of Jewish living and Jewish faith principles. How fortunate we are to have received and realized all that we know and believe. Therefore, the reading should be "how fortunate are the poor in spirit."

"The poor in spirit." What is the source of this saying? Does it mean literally poor people without means? The reading in Luke 6:20 would imply that thought. If so, then the Hebrew or Aramaic source may have referred to *aniyim* (poor) or *anavim* (humble), which may reflect a historical reality. During the days of Sellucid rule, the poor—in contrast to the wealthy or powerful—remained true to the ancient faith of Israel. Therefore, our text would imply, happy are those who don't give up the faith in hopes of receiving the gifts of the ruling power.

As for poverty itself, Judaism didn't see any special virtue in self-imposed poverty, but rather poverty, as all of life's circumstances, is an opportunity for spiritual development, the belief being that, through poverty, one may be moved toward repentence (Lachs, p. 71).

"Those who mourn"—this refer to *avelei Tzion*—those who mourn for Zion and the destruction of the Temple. In the Sermon on the Mount, Jesus is seen as the great comforter. Life must continue. Our Sages said, "One shouldn't mourn incessantly, nor should there be any tradition imposed on the community which might be observed more in breach than in the practice."

"Blessed are the meek"—read, "happy are the meek." The meek are the *aniyim* mentioned above. In the post-Hebrew Bible literature (Jubliees, Enoch, etc.), one finds references to the meek, the *aniyim*, as well as others, inheriting the earth. Thus, I agree with Lachs that verse 5 may be a response to a scribe's marginal note. The mourners, the meek, those who hunger and thirst for righteousness, will receive the reward.

Rabbi Tanchum ben Rabbi Chanilai spoke of those who starve themselves for the sake of the Torah in this world, hoping they will be rewarded in the World to Come. It's an eschatological teaching, and it may be a bridge between Jewish-Rabbinic sources and Matthew-Luke.

"Blessed are the merciful"—read, "happy are the merciful." In the Septuagint, *tzedakah* (righteous) and *chesed* (mercy) are both translated as "righteousness." The Rabbis taught, "he who shows mercy or righteousness to his fellow creatures obtains mercy or righteousness from Heaven." The black brush of excommunication was used freely in some first-century circles. This text, "happy are the merciful," may refer to such circles. Thus, if one shows mercy rather than use the black brush, they will be rewarded. The Hebrew original may have been, as Lachs suggests, *ashrei ha-muchramim ki hemah yirachmu*, which means "happy are they who extend mercy, for it will be extended to them." Happy are they that are excommunicated, for they shall receive mercy (merciful treatment in their new belief).

"Pure in heart"—Hebrew, *barei livam*, see Psalms 24:4 and 73:1. It means "sincere ones," hence "happy are the sincere ones."

"For they shall see God"—in the Rabbinic tradition, seeing God is seeing the *Shekhinah*. The *Shekhinah* and God are synonymous. The *Shekhinah* is another aspect of God, the embracing, compassionate side of God. The moment of such seeing occurs when one "binds up the wounded of heart, proclaim release to the captives, liberation to the imprisoned" (Isaiah 61:1). Seeing the *Shekhinah* is a reward for the performance of such *mitzvot*. "If a man gives a coin to a beggar, he is worthy of receiving the *Shekhinah* (the Divine Presence)" (Leviticus Rabba 23:13).

"Happy are the peacemakers, for they shall be called sons of God." In the *Ethics of the Fathers*, we read: "Hillel said, 'Be of the disciples of Aaron, loving peace and pursuing peace, loving mankind, and bringing them to the Torah'" (Mishnah Avot 1:12). The pursuance of peace and peaceful solutions to life's dilemmas was an early rabbinic concept. Perhaps Matthew was aware of this tradition and urged it upon "Christian" followers. As for being called "the sons of God," see Deuteronomy 1:30–31 "for God is forever protecting you as a shepherd tends his sheep. Thus, if you do God's work, then you are surely one of God's children."

"Happy are those who are persecuted for righteousness' sake." Happy are you when men revile and persecute you and utter all kinds of evil against you, falsely on My account. Lachs suggests the reading should be "those who are persecuted for their allegiance to the *tzadiq*, the righteous one." It can be compared to the teacher of the Dead Sea community. In later Hasidic literature, hasidim saw themselves persecuted for allegiance to the *tzadiq* they followed. Therefore, we see here the beginnings of the this idea: Ofttimes our being persecuted is due to our allegiances.

"Being reviled on my account" was reality. Early Christians were persecuted and reviled on account of their allegiances, the ultimate reward yet to be realized.

Isi Ben-Yehudah taught, "Why do scholars die before their time? Because they despise themselves" (Avot de Rabi Natan 30).

In our western culture, humility is a central virtue. Our pedagogy urges the muting of our selves. Children should be seen and not heard. Oftentimes as adults we are irked by the precocious child. If a child shows signs of brilliance, we seldom cater to him or her. He or she is left to their own devices. This in turn leads to boredom on the part of the bright one, or possibly withdrawal from life with all its attendant problems. We've created systems known as Special Education for them. We isolate them from their peers. This in turn makes an impression on the less gifted: the gifted ones must be so strange that it is better for them to be kept apart from "normal" people.

In my counseling practice, I've met many extremely brilliant individuals who felt isolated, not accepted by society as a whole, their brilliance having stood them in no good stead.

Thus Isi ben Yehudah was correct in his maxim. Scholars—brilliant, knowledgeable people—who see further than the accepted norms, who raise questions about all of life's problems, attitudes, and approaches, feel the sting of isolation and take into unto themselves the criticisms of the many and hasten their own demises.

Magiei bayit be-vayit sadeh v-sadeh yaqrivu ad efes maqom ve-hoshavtem levadchem be-qerev ha-aretz

Those who add house to house and join field to field, til there is room but none but you to dwell in the land (Isaiah 5:8).

In every generation, there is a culprit whose hunger for owning property or other things is never sated. Such people seldom ask themselves, "What is driving me? Why am I so hungry for things? Why can't I calm my hunger by addressing it and truly understand its source, namely, something in my own inner soul?" In the Creation story, we were told that everything was created according to its own kind, provided with a mechanism for its own reproduction and survival, and therefore God, the Creator, said it was good. What applies to nature applies to the rest of us, too. If only we would address the treasure that is ourselves, and completely understand, then much of our unbridled hunger would be laid to rest. If I can hear the music in my head, then why must I be drawn to the noises of the world? If I can relate to my inner physician, then why must I be so dependent on artificially produced chemicals? If only I could tap into the innate love that resides in my soul, I wouldn't feel the need to prove my strength or existence by conquering others.

In time, according to the text, God the Creator had lost his taste for the human. He saw "man's great wickedness on the Earth," and "every plan devised by his mind was nothing but evil all the time." "The Lord said, 'I regret that I made thee.'"

But Noah found favor with the Lord." Scripture's emphasis seems to be that it's never a total loss. There is always a remnant worth saving. After the flood, Noah is told "Never again will I doom the Earth because of man, since the decisions of man's mnd are evil from his youth, nor will I ever again destroy every living being, as I have done."

From that prehistoric moment to the present, the spiritual lesson seems to be that life will never end. Catastrophes may occur, but life will never cease altogether. Predictions of great apocalyptic moments may abound, but life will still go on. The destroyer of life is not God, but the human driven by selfishness and greed, by unsatisfied appetites forever coveting that which is not his, saying to himself, "I have been given the sacred task to cleanse the world" meanwhile bringing destruction down upon city inhabitants.

We humans haven't abided by our covenant with God. We tried to outwit Him, to behave as if we were the world's creators and shapers instead of saying it is with God's help that we are assured of our success. God doesn't seek the demise of the human; rather, He seeks only to have us return to the divine premises of love, care, and compassion that underpins human existence.

*

Genesis 6 is a review of the human condition. It had become a mixture of the eternal and the now. For some reason, the barrier that separated the waters of the above from those below didn't seem to apply to human behavior. In the human, the apex of creation, such fine distinctions didn't exist. Instead, our text tells us in a metaphysical way, the divine—the *benei Elohim*—beings comingled with the early human and produced offspring, in other words, partly human, partly divine. Such hybrids disturbed the divine plan.

When the Creator considered the fate of disobedient Adam and said, "Now that he knows the difference between the good (the natural) and the *ra* (unnatural), he may eat of the fruit of the Tree of Life and be assured of eternal life." Therefore, he banished Adam from the Garden. The separation between the divine and the human must continue.

In the incident of the divine beings commingling with the humans, the same issue arose. The separation between the divine and the human had been breached. As an outcome, the human's tenure was limited. Adam was cursed, "You shall live by the sweat of your brow" was reaffirmed. The human was left to live by his own devices.

The human seemed to ignore the divine breath resident within him since creation. When that breath no longer played a role, man deteriorated. The human was driven by power, by an urge to dominate, to preempt, to say "might is right." God is troubled by it, saying, "I regret my creations." But Noah (rest, calmness, serenity, balance) found favor in the Creator's eyes.

One Way Jesus

Thomas said to him, "Lord, we do not know where you are going. How can we know the way?"
Jesus said to him, "I am the way, and the truth, and the life. No one comes to the Father except through me (John 14:5-6).

Countless Jews and Muslims have suffered from the loving hands of Christians because of this sentence: No one comes to God except through Christ. It is doubting Thomas who asks the question in John's gospel and who receives the answer. We people of faith, Christians, Jews, and Muslim, Democrats, Republicans, Communists, Liberals, Conservatives, human rights activists, ecologists, military, we all can relate to this sentence: there is only one way to a better life! Without conviction many of us would not do what we are doing.

But my voice is only one voice. We can only sing in harmony as long as we sing soft enough to hear the other voices in the choir.   *DJT*

Va-yerah Adonai et kol asher asah ve-hineh tov meod

*And God saw all that he had made,
and behold, it was very good (Genesis 1:31).*

The Sages of old were never deterred by omissions, detractions, and even contradictions in the biblical text. They forever sought to understand the phrases that we would otherwise say, "Well, that's the way it's written." Rabbi Eleazar, commenting on the phrase, "And God saw all that he had made, and behold, it was very good," said "Here was restored the omission of 'it was very good' of the second day, because death was created on that day." The sensitivity of the Sages is beyond measure. Rabbi Eleazar was asking, why was the phrase "it was very good" omitted on the second day? He said it was "Because death was created on that day."

The Zohar 1:46b said, "The Angel of Death was created on the Second Day, along with all of the angels of judgment." Death and judgment, always produced a side effect, often bringing in their wake sorrow, pain, and suffering. And to Rabbi Eleazar and other sages, suffering, though it may be needed for growth, can never be considered good.

Can suffering be avoided in this world? Must it be considered a negative quality? Why can't we say that suffering is a platform from which all that is good and creative springs? Is it possible to bring anything into this world without some pain and suffering? When you have a morsel of food, apply heat to it to cook it. I'm sure the native ingredients, if given half a chance, would say, "Ouch. You're causing me pain. It hurts." Suffering is real, and just as darkness is part of the day, so suffering is a part of life. But how can one immunize oneself from the pain that suffering causes? Perhaps by saying, "The suffering was just another step that cannot be avoided." You have to cross the ditch to get to the dry land.

In the *Ethics of the Fathers* we read, "Be deliberate in judgment." This statement was debated in the ancient academies. One Sage said, "It means one should take time in rendering judgment." Another, Aba Shaul, said, "it means they interpreted." This is the key to understanding rabbinic literature. Interpretation. Never say the final word has been spoken on any issue. Each of us is bestowed with the breath of God in us, and has the freedom to interpret and to act. To affirm and assent to such-and-such is the answer for my life. Whether it be in gender roles, or in our relations with others, ultimately, *I* am the actor, *I* am the director, *I* am the playwright for my life.

Even then it follows that we cannot always appeal to traditions, to writings of previous generations, and say "by this and with this we must abide." Judaism as we understand it admonishes us, with every part of you in tow, serve God. For God reveals Himself according to our power of understanding Him. At one moment, our soul is functioning on the purest level, at others, at the level tinged by the stirrings and consternations of the world around us. Ultimately, we come back to the major premise of our tradition: "Love (be bound, tied, hinged) *Adonai* your God." Not a God defined for all times but one who is in a constant state of revelation.

Of course, the second command is simple. Just as you love God unconditionally, extend the same grace to any human you may meet.

What transpired when the *nachash* befriended the woman? Folklore abounds with many tales and theories. The woman, later named Eve, saw the *nachash* eating the forbidden fruit of the tree, and she took a bite and delighted in its taste. The *nachash* moved closer and engaged her in conversation. He tried to convince her of the legitimacy of eating the fruit. If it was the Creator's intent for her not to eat of it, why did He create it? She accepted with alacrity his logic. In a few moments, legend has it, she was intrigued by his small talk, and they became intimate. The *nachash* impregnated her with his seed, and Qayin was the outcome of this adventure, one who wasn't obedient by nature, one who lived by his astounding power, by his instincts, never bridling them. The tradition of the paternity of Qayin was well-known in medieval circles. It was often cited. People said, "We're faced with a problem. Could Adam, the naive one who didn't question Eve, have been the father of the one whose nature was to destroy, and not to build, humankind?" This links up to the later legend of Qayin proposing to Hevel, "Let's divide the world up between us."

Hesiani

"[The nachash*] enticed me (Genesis 3:13)."*

That was Eve's defense. Bearing in mind the previously quoted legend, "Eve saw him, the *nachash,* eat the forbidden fruit, and she followed suit" the enticement was prolonged." One *midrash* said, the *nachash* had an inner debate within himself. He resented Adam's creation. He was *arum,* the most *arum,* pristine of all created beings. It meant he was privy to all knowledge, and resented Adam being considered the culmination of all of the created beings. He saw himself as on the same plane as all the other higher created beings. *Malachim,* angels, *Adonai's* helpers, were created on the second day. Thus, he claimed for himself the right to challenge *Adonai Elohim,* the Creator of all beings. Since, said the *nachash,* I draw from the same well of wisdom as *Adonai Elohim,* I have the right to entice Adam and Eve, the parents of living humans, and lessen their power, lest they overtake me. His plot was via Eve to bring about Adam's downfall. By eating the forbidden fruit in front of her, he attracted her attention, and after much conversation, became intimate with her, creating the destructive spawn, Qayin.

Adam and Eve were expelled from the garden. Their punishment was theirs alone, not for the rest of human existence. They would wander, yes. Eve would suffer the pangs of childbirth. Adam will live by the sweat of his brow. Constant enmity will exist between the *nachash* and humanity. The notion that 'By Adam's fall suffer we all'" isn't expressed by the text. The key to human behavior is stated later, when Qayin was trying to arrive at a meaning of and for life, and he was told, "Sin crouches at the door, and you can overcome it." Each individual is capable of choosing, and no one is eternally condemned, needing another to save him.

Where Do Babies Come From?

So God created humankind in his image, in the image of God he created them; male and female he created them (Gen 1:27).

Where do babies come from? - When God created the first human being he or she was both a man and a woman in one body. But then the human felt lonely, and the Creator took a bone from the body. By losing a part the human became a boy. And out of the bone God made a girl. And this is why boys are chasing girls and girls long for boys. They desire to be complete again. And each time a baby is born their desire is fulfilled and the two, the father and the mother, become one body in the child.   *DJT*

Va-yetze Qayin me-lifnei Adonai va-yeshev ba-aretz Nod qidmat Eiden

*Qayin left the presence of the Lord
and settled in the land of Nod, east of Eden.*

It would seem from this text that the biblical tradition was that the "cradle of civilization" is east of Eden, the land of Nod (wanderers). From its earliest passages, the text favored the wanderers, not the settled ones. This is partly due to reality, for we know from our studies that the earliest migrant humans dwelled at riverbeds, behind natural barriers and caves. Each migration had its reason: sources of water; later, navigational routes; the need to cover vast expanses where game and produce could be found; and caves and shelters where one could be protected from the elements. This led to the formation of alliances between the "wanderers" and whatever (or whomever) they discovered in natural sequences. For instance, the stars and moon acted as guides for the seasons: planting and harvesting. The sun was relied upon for its warmth, heating rays, and power over plant life. Caves provided shelter from carnivores who ate beast and human alike. In the caves, one often finds recorded history's tale, people's myths, and above all, the political establishments, dotting the world's surface.

Qayin, in his new domicile, sets about producing the next generation; in generations following Qayin and Hevel, an attempt was made (according to the text) to establish human enclaves. In the names given to those whole followed Qayin and Hevel, we can discern the outlines of these.

Qayin's first offspring is Chanokh (Enoch). *Ch-N-Kh* in Hebrew means learning, education. This is the first step toward passing down the wisdom of the "ancient ones," hoping thereby to enrich the city built by Qayin and his list of offspring. In the story of Qayin, and in abbreviated form, of Adam and Chavah, one sees the outlines of emerging civilization, both nomadic and later settled. On the settled side there have been found metal artifacts and harvesting tools that provided power independent of God. At first, the flexing of human muscles was a matter of individual acts, but then we find pre-emptive attempts leading to violence and bloodshed. At this point, *Adonai* intervenes, as if to say, "If you want to go your own individual way, go for it. For I gave you the special breath, which is the source of your personal individuation, intelligence, and self-fulfillment. But once you take upon yourselves the role of God, no longer subject to limitations but forever asserting yourself at the expense of others, I call a halt."

In Genesis 4:26 we read "A son was also born to Seth, and he called him by the name Enosh. It was then that the name of *Adonai* was invoked." This verse is followed by Adam's genealogy (Gen. 5): Adam was created, made by *Elohim*. On the day he was created, his appearance or likeness was that of *Elohim*, the difference being Adam was a human being containing male and female characteristics (5:1–2). His genealogy is limited; neither Qayin nor Hevel are listed as Adam's children, only Seth. This is, according to the text, the true human chain. As we read in 4:26, Seth gave birth to Enosh (Enoch). In that generation, humans attested their relationship to *Adonai* as a) They were made in *Adonai's* or Elohim's image; b) In their identity with God, humans accepted or rejected divine influence, guidance, and authority. According to the text, two strains of likeness to *Adonai* Elohim appeared, one leading to Chanokh (Enoch) who walked with God (5:22), and the other to the members of Noach's generation. Noach's generation, we are told, was corrupt (6:9). In an attempt to explain these two strains, the sages cite the source of corruption as the mixture of the sacred with the profane, the divine beings (6:2) intermingled with the human, and this admixture produced the corrupt generation. In other words, the text is warning us that once the division between divine and human is confused, dire consequences may ensue.

Genesis 6 is a review of the human behavior condition. It had become a mixture of the eternal and the now. For some reason, the barrier that separated the waters of above from those below didn't seem to apply to human behavior.

No Regard

Now Abel was a keeper of sheep, and Cain a tiller of the ground. ...
And the LORD had regard for Abel and his offering, but for Cain and
his offering he had no regard (Genesis 4:2.5).

The story goes that Cain decided to stay home to better be able to provide for his family. He may have had to look after his elderly parents, Adam and Eve, because Abel was on the road too much. Cain is the rigorous scholar, who works at his desk; the loyal priest, who tends to the dwindling number of parishioners in his rural congregation; the faithful husband, who never took chances with other women. And yet, for Cain and his offering, God had no regard.   *DJT*

U-vacharta be-chayim

Choose life (Deut. 30:19)!

Our Jewish tradition places great stress and importance on life. It was a radical departure from the Egyptian emphasis on death. It was common practice in Egyptian circles to build great monuments, tomb-cities, for the facilitation of the deceased (royalty and others) to go from the land of the living to the realm of the dead. As a reaction to this emphasis on death, Moses, the great teacher and lawgiver stated in his final address, "Choose life." Choosing life meant adopting an array of positive life-giving acts called *mitzvot*, the belief being that the system of *mitzvot* is the creative method for life giving life.

Among these *mitzvot* are blessings. We're taught that one should recite one hundred blessings per day, for each blessing has a creative aspect. Not only does it affirm God's truth and goodness, but it also stirs the reciter to focus on life given to us by God. For example, a blessing recited each morning praises God for having instilled in certain animals and birds the discernment to distinguish night from day. The purpose of this blessing is to affirm an ancient notion that God the creator, in His wisdom, created a universe that can be known and studied, unlike other creation stories, which placed in the hands of the various forces called gods control over the universe. Life was dependent on their moods rather than on laws built into the natural system. The Jewish thesis was that certain birds are granted the power of discernment and of time. The human is endowed with the power of reason and free choice. The world is here; its law governs it. But the choice is yours: will you live by these laws, or will you try to beat the game? Thus Moses says, *u-vacharta,* choose life, choose to live by its measure of time, wellness, and serenity, or face the consequences.

Ha-Kenani lashevet be-aretz ha-zot

The Canaanites lived in the land (Judges 1:27).

The term "Canaanites" is all-encompassing. It refers to the indigenous population of the land to which Abram had been directed. In the Torah, we have scattered references to this population, their way of life, their cultic practices and social structures. To completely envision them, one has to consult extraneous material, for many times, when the Torah admonishes us not to follow their practices, we are only given pointed hints. The way of Abram was a) To find his own vision, "the way you are meant to be"; and b) To introduce a new approach to life, peacefully, into the Canaanite scene.

What was Abram's path? The Zohar, the textbook of Qabalah and Jewish mysticism says, "Abram sought to draw near to the Blessed Holy One, and He was drawn near to him." Rabbi Huna said, "From the Torah, from the Prophets and the Writings, it can be demonstrated that one can be led on the path that one wishes to take." The Zohar tradition, driven by the need to discover the mystery behind life, always sought to find the essence, the special something, that leads one to the path of God. *Tiferet*—righteousness and *rachamim*—compassion, are the cornerstones of the path that leads to God. The stubborn-hearted, those who shun right-eousness—*tzedeq* or *tiferet*—shun God. The Holy Blessed One (God) is called *tiferet*, beauty and glory. His other name is *tzedaqah*—righteousness. His feminine side, the *Shekhinah* is also known as *tzedaqah*, as righteous acts. Abraham, says the Zohar, through his acts of *tzedaqah*, approached the *Shekhinah*, God's feminine side, and became known as one of God's and the *Shekhinah*'s adherents. Those who avoid *tzedeq* and *tzedaqah* avoid peace. The *yesod*, the foundation, or in Qabalis-tic terms the *phallus*, brings *tzedeq* and *tzedaqah* together.

Our Sages teach, one should recite one hundred *berakhot* (blessings) every day. In other words, for whatever occurs in your life, bless God, for the power of God, the endless power of life, is ever-occuring, never ceasing, never holding back. Thus, whatever happens to us, God is there. Whenever we are ready to stand back and say, "In Your hands, I place my spirit and my body, too. *Adonai* is with me and I am not afraid," the God-power is activated, and solutions to our im-mediate problems appear.

As the Psalmist said, "Look here, the Keeper of Israel (or for that matter, of the Universe) neither slumbers nor sleeps." Even though the Keeper is forever attendant, he seems with-drawn when we try in our naiveté to act as if we are the Keeper ourselves, when we hesitate in admitting that there is a higher power in the universe waiting for our summons. To be able to say "I place my body and spirit in Your hands," your full presence is required. When we are willing to mute our egos and activate our spirits and our souls, the "resident place" of the God we seek in our lives, it is at that point that God appears and his presence is felt.

Adonai oz le-amo yiten. Adonai yivarekh et amo ba-shalom.

God gives strength to His people. God blesses His people with peace (Psalms 27:11).

When we Jews use the name *Adonai* for God, we are referring to God in God's most ultimate state. In the Book of Exodus, in the early part of the Exodus story, we are told "*Elohim* spoke to Moses." According to Jewish tradition, the name *Elohim* refers to that aspect of the Creator that assures us that there is a just and reasonable existence for the world and all that is in it. In other words, there are built-in rules, regulations, and other relationships, so that the world will never disintegrate. In this verse, *Elohim* says to Moses, "I've appeared to your ancestors as *El-Shaddai*, which means God the Provider." Thus, whenever, we enter a Jewish home, we find a *mezuzah* affixed to the door, and the letter *Shin* on the case, referring to *El-Shaddai*, the one who provides. *Elohim* continues, "But my name, *Adonai*, I've never shared with them. At this point, I'm sharing it with you, and I hope you will carry forth my mission and bring it forth to these enslaved people."

Adonai signals never-ending existence. *Adonai* is *Ein Sof* (without end). It's to *Ein Sof* that we aspire as humans; every one of us is on a journey. Some climb mountains, others cross valleys, and still others ford streams. Our tradition teaches us that if you have *Adonai*, the *Ein Sof*, in mind, no matter what you face, *oz* (strength) is given to you. Thus *oz le-amo yiten*, he gives strength to his people. And when you have placed yourself within the fortunate state of faith, you will find the peace that knows no bounds. *Adonai yivarekh et amo ba-shalom.* Adonai blesses his followers with peace.

Sehma beni musar avikha ve-torat imekha (Proverbs 1:8). The author of Proverbs attempted in his or her own way to provide us with a scheme for righteous living. He said that to live the righteous life, one must adopt certain parameters. First and foremost, you have to accept in a loving way the world from which you stem. You can make your own adjustments, you can fine-tune it, but to cut yourself away from it entirely leaves you stranded in the midst of nowhere. There are certain things in life that are given: our DNA, our soul-message, our traits, and our tendencies.

I may be a disciplined person; I will therefore act one way.

I may be a sensitive person; I'll behave another way.

But whatever way I choose, I cannot hope to truly prosper if there isn't a relationship to the root base from which I stem. Therefore, listen, my child, to the *musar* of your father and to the *Torah* of your mother, for they are the beginning of your existence.

Mi-pi olelim ve-yonqim yosadita oz

From the mouths of infants and toddlers comes eternal truth
(Psalms 8:3).

Carl Jung once said that the truths that we know by the time our egos are formed at age three are truer than true.

There is an ancient Jewish legend that says that before a child is born, the soul designated for that child is all-knowing. In the course of birth, something happens, and it forgets its knowledge, therefore needing a remedial life.

Many of us recall the famous tale of Isaac Bashevis Singer, the soul who got through and whose wisdom was not held back. In fact, again according to Jewish folklore, the indentation under your nose is the spot where the angel in charge of souls made his impression, thus what had been put into the nostril of the first human is held back from more recent candidates for human life.

Jewish folklore has always attempted to answer the great puzzles of life. How come some children know more than others? Why are some on the brink of being geniuses, while others can't pull themselves up out of the dark pits of ignorance? Folklore tries to answer these questions by saying, "Everything is *bashert*" or by placing the blame on the pressure of the angel when the soul was about to enter its designated body. Perhaps there are other answers. Jung is correct in saying that children are the wisest of us all. They haven't yet been affected or infected by the tainted winds of the worlds that surround them. They haven't yet attended schools whose sole purpose in life is to make you fit into the established norms of society. It's the rare teacher who listens to the child and is guided by him or her. More often than not, it is the child who is molded by the teachers. The Psalmist, in stating this phrase, "From the mouths of infants" knew the untarnished power and realized it's lost when the child is made to march to someone else's tune. Therefore, in a more subtle way, the Jewish tradition is correct again when it says, in the book of Proverbs, "Teach or train the child according to his or her own way, and not of another."

A Reader's Digest *Version*

But there are also many other things that Jesus did; if every one of them were written down, I suppose that the world itself could not contain the books that would be written (John 21:25).

In the last sentence of the canonical Four Gospel Collection an editor tells us that he or she did not set out to produce a complete record of Jesus' accomplishments, just a selection. If one attempted to publish everything known about Jesus, the world could not hold all the books. Four books are enough; something like a reader's digest. This open record leaves room for our own spiritual experience and for our own struggle to understand. *DJT*

Ha-zoreim be-dimah be-rinah yiqtzoru

Those who plant in tears will harvest with joy (Psalms 126:5).

Life provides us with strange moments and stranger partners. We seldom choose them; rather they seem to come our way. What is their origin? Can it be traced?

Many studies have shown that during each moment of our lives, we send messages far and wide. When we think of someone far away, or pray for someone far away, and wish for his or her well-being, we release a form of energy that can prove to be a healer or a reliever of pain and stress. When we wish upon a star, the wish sends out power of its own, newly created power. The wish becomes a fulfilled dream.

No one seems to know the source of such power. The Psalmist said, "We may sow with tears, with sadness, yet reap in a joyful, serene way." Transformations of energy are continuous, creation of healing vibes never ceases. It's as if to say, that the Torah's statement that we are the Creator's is surrogate also means that we too can speak, and it will come into being.

We return to our original question: "Who and what sends us to the place where our sought-for partner can be found?" How do we know we're in the right place? Who directs us there?

In Jewish tradition, you have the concept of *bashert*. It means "the designated one," as if to say, "From our moment of birth, we have known who it may be," and our inner compass proceeds to bring us to that individual. Some of us dismiss these notions and say that they are sheer superstition. Are they? If all of life is connected, and if the author of life is the same for all of us, then why can't we accept the notion that the spark of the author lying within us is also the tool that brings us to whom we must meet?

Mah lekha ha-yam ki tanus ha-Yarden tisov le-achor

What is with you, Sea, that you turn away, or with you, O Jordan, that you reverse direction (Psalms 114:5)?

When one reads Psalms, or any biblical poetry, one is confronted by the poet's sense of awe and wonder. Nature, God, and history are all sources of wonder. In the above-quoted phrase, the Psalmist is addressing the wonder of it all: "Why did the sea retreat, and why did the river Jordan change its course?" In studying these texts, scholars try to place them in historical context. One can never truly reach a universal conclusion, though. One thing can be said about biblical prose and poetry: it concentrates on the awesomeness of God's presence in this world.

The Psalmist implies that the sea and the Jordan had no choice. Facing God and his understanding of the moment, they gave way to His power and to His sense of the moment. Those who lived by his point of view were rescued. Those who undermined God's understanding of the moment were removed from the face of the earth.

The Psalmist, whoever he or she may have been, is addressing him- or herself to a moment of history: The Exodus from Egypt. How shall it be viewed? How did God relate to it? Was it influenced by Him? Is it a mark of nature to respond to Him? Or is nature governed by its own rules, separate from God? This uncertainty is resolved by the Psalmist in asking, "Why did the great sea behave as it did, and the Jordan, the great divide, behave in its way?" Both occurrences attest to that which is beyond them and us: God.

Salvation for All

Let it be known to you then that this salvation of God has been sent to the Gentiles; they will listen (Acts 28:28).

Why is it that so many more Greek speaking Jews, Jews who lived among the Gentiles, recognized Jesus as the Christ? Luke writes in Greek for Greek speaking Jews. It takes Luke two volumes, his 'Gospel' and his 'Acts of the Apostles,' to explain to us what happened; how the movement, which was started by a conservative rabbi in rural Galilee, found its way into the hearts of so many people living abroad: people like us and people like Paul, whom Jesus most certainly would have considered a liberal.   *DJT*

Hineh lo yanum ve-lo yishan shomer Yisrael

The guardian of Israel neither slumbers nor sleeps (Psalms 121:4).

The guardian of Israel. God has always been seen in that light. This was expressed in ancient times in many ways. Night and day He is at your side. No matter what you may face, He is there with you.

After the Second World War, many people, both survivors and observers of the Holocaust, refused to recite this Psalm. They said, "For one who is always there, He proved to be quite scarce in the days of the worldwide Holocaust." For you see, the horror of World War II affected all of mankind. No one was safe from the terror that lurked by day and the fear by night. The destruction touched every continent, and plans were afoot for the conquest of the entire Western hemisphere. By 1932, everyone was aware of National Socialism's plan for world conquest. Its allies in Italy, Spain, and Japan (and elsewhere) had agreed with the Germans on a plan for world conquest, and each supported their "allies" in all undertakings. Africa was affected, Asia was compromised, and plans that were never put into effect, when revealed, sealed the fate of North, Central, and South America. Australia and New Zealand were also on the conqueror's horizon. So where was the guardian who neither slept nor slumbered?

I've heard many answers to this question. Only one rings true. We always say, "Forewarned is forearmed." Hitler, Moussolini, Stalin, and Franco openly revealed their plans. We humans didn't respond. Many of us joined them. God cannot be blamed for our oversight. It's a weak answer, but true. As in Egypt, when the propitious moment arrived, He responded.

Stories of Adam

For Adam was formed first, then Eve; and Adam was not deceived, but the woman was deceived and became a transgressor (1 Timothy 2:13-14).

In 1838 Joseph Smith, the prophet of the Church of Jesus Christ of Latter-day Saints, through divine revelation, was shown the place where Adam lived and built an altar after he left the Garden Eden. Adam-ondi-Ahman is located in Daviess County, Missouri, about 70 miles northeast of Kansas City. Although the altar withstood the test of time for thousands of years, it has disintegrated completely during the past 150. Our Christian, Jewish, and Muslim experience seems to be a mixture of both naïve and heartfelt readings of Jewish traditions, personal experiences of the Divine, and historically questionable events.   *DJT*

Halanu atah o-litzarenu?

Are you one of ours, or one of our enemies (Joshua 5:13)?

We're told Joshua, of biblical fame, met a stranger and posed the question: "Are you one of us, or are you one of them (our detractors, our enemies)?" It seemed to him that one must always belong to either one camp or the other. He was wary of the straddlers, the me-toos of this world, yet the me-toos were the *erev rav,* the joiners, the non-Israelites that appeared at the covenant ceremony.

In Jewish tradition, we are constantly faced with the problem of viewing everyone as either "we" or "they." It led to much misunderstanding. The rare ones among us were willing to say, "Even these days there are many who see themselves as our allies" or, as was said in previous generations, "friends of God."

What can be said of us, the Jews, can be said of many others. Our history teaches us that the circle of the "we" is wider than we think, and the circle of "them" is lessening.

Our century calls for bridges that bring all humans together and for filling in the chasms that separate us. It calls for discarding of emotional and philosophical notions that point fingers, cast aspersions, denigrate, and negate one another. The lesson is found in our area of common experience, and belief is becoming greater than the realm of disbelief. The challenge is not to concentrate on our detractors, but to find our affirmers.

Mi Ladonai Elai

Whoever is for God, [come] with me (I Maccabees 2:27)!

We're told that the triggering factor in the Maccabeean rebellion were these three words: "Whoever allies himself with *Adonai*, follow me." Matitiyahu (Matathias) uttered them. His zealousness is lauded in prayers recited on Chanukah. His audacity has been admired throughout the generations.

Legend would have us believe such calls based on pure faith (and not on planned military campaigns) can melt any human resistance. Can this be an eternal model? When faced with harsh reality, can we find the strength that overcomes all obstacles in calls to faith? Or was it a one-time affair, never to be repeated? How shall we address life's impediments? By faith alone, or by faith backed up by well-thought-out plans of action?

The Sages say little about Chanukah. In their skepticism, they look askance at the miraculous claims of the Maccabeean heritage. Can it be that their adage, "Don't rely on miracles, signs, and portents" is the truer approach to life?

It seems to us that the Rabbis who are constantly seeking balance in life arrive at the conclusion that although we don't rely on miracles, we also don't deny the possibility of their occurrence. One never knows whether an occurrence is a sign (*nes*) or a suspension of nature (miracle).

Approaching life that way, one is ready to accept whatever may arrive, thus leading to this statement of the Rabbis: "One blesses God for the good and for the not-so-good, for both the proven intervention and for the hoped-for intervention of God."

A Cloud of Witnesses

Therefore, since we are surrounded by so great a cloud of witnesses, let us also lay aside every weight and the sin that clings so closely, and let us run with perseverance the race that is set before us, looking to Jesus the pioneer and perfecter of our faith, who for the sake of the joy that was set before him endured the cross, disregarding its shame, and has taken his seat at the right hand of the throne of God. Consider him who endured such hostility against himself from sinners, so that you may not grow weary or lose heart. In your struggle against sin you have not yet resisted to the point of shedding your blood (Letter to the Hebrews 12:1-4).

We are surrounded by a great cloud of witnesses. Some, like the writer of this sermon, testify to the redemptive power of Jesus' death. But all of us are united in the effort to make a difference by struggling against sin with perseverance and to the point of shedding blood, in faithful hopes that, at the end of our race, there will be joy.   *DJT*

Martyrs: Who Are They?

Every generation has its litany of martyrs. If you read the Yom Kippur liturgy, it is a collection of martyr stories. We suspect that the original Yom Kippur liturgy was in fact a martyrology. These are the giants of the faith. They gave their lives for God, Torah, and Israel. In Leviticus, we read the Yom Kippur temple liturgy. It includes the sending of the goats: one to heaven, the other to Azalzel. The latter bore the sins of the community. It was a communal martyr.

In later generations, the martyrology takes on other forms. The first generation after the destruction of the Temple had its group of martyrs: the ten *charugei malkhut*, who were killed by the Roman government because they practiced the forbidden faith. By the time of the Crusades, there was a legion of martyrs, those who refused to bow to the cross, who gave their lives for the faith, such as those who were incinerated (the Jews of York, England, etc.) or tortured by zealous Christians, intent on making Europe and elsewhere the bastions of Christian faith. The same is true in Islam; there were martyrs galore.

What prompts martyrdom? One, my love for the One whom I adore and worship. I give my life as a gift to the Deity. Another cause is the idea that in martyrdom, the existence of my soul is elevated to a higher plane. A third reason is the belief that the martyrs' souls have been given entrée and access. They stand before the celestial throne, a feat seldom accomplished by ordinary mortals (except for Elijah, Enoch, *et al.*)

In the traditional Jewish marriage ceremony, the couple is blessed with *ahavah, achvah, shalom,* and *reiut. Ahavah* (usually translated as "love") means linkage. May your new relationship be so strong that you feel linked as strongly as the links of a chain are to each other. *Achvah,* may your relationship be as meaningful as a kinship-relationship, as if you are of the same cloth, brother and sister. *Shalom,* may your experience be peace, harmony, and completeness in all you undertake; and *reiut,* may you know the true meaning of friendship. May you feel toward one another the true bond of friendship, the kind of bond we speak of when we say, "Be linked to your friend as you would be to yourself."

It is the quintessential blessing. What else can we ask for in the realm of relationships? This formula of *ahavah, achvah, shalom,* and *reiut* forms the ultimate four pillars on which the universe rests: love, brotherliness, peace, and true friendship. It's a formula not only for marriage and for married life, but also for social harmony.

INDEX

Jewish Scripture

Genesis 1:1 94
Genesis 1:27 186
Genesis 1:31 182
Genesis 2:7 43
Genesis 3:9 150
Genesis 4:2.5 189
Genesis 6:11 65
Genesis 7:23 67
Genesis 8:12-13 67
Genesis 12 98
Exodus 19:6 39
Exodus 20:8 167
Exodus 20:17 37
Leviticus 11: 44. 40
Leviticus 26:3 147
Numbers 14:20 84
Deuteronomy 28:6 55
Deuteronomy. 30:19 190
Joshua 5:13 202
Judges 1:27 191
Judges 10:16 140
Judges 11:39-40 146
II Samuel 7:18 93
II Kings 14:27 91
Nehemiah 5:1-8 47
Song of Songs 1:5-7 45
Job 1:8 53
Psalms 2:1-6 79
Psalms 8:3 195
Psalms 9:11 26
Psalms 9:11 80
Psalms 14:1 111
Psalms 19:1 109

Psalms 23 107
Psalms 23:1 22
Psalms 23:4 41
Psalms 23:4 136
Psalms 27:11 193
Psalms 29:11 11
Psalms 29:4–6 156
Psalms 35:2 52
Psalms 35:10 128
Psalms 36:2. 119
Psalms 37:1 118
Psalms 56:4 96
Psalms 83:2 105
Psalms 94:3 33
Psalms 103:1 61
Psalms 114:5 198
Psalms 118:5 29
Psalms 121:1-2 124
Psalms 121:4 134
Psalms 121:4 200
Psalms 126:5 197
Psalms 133:1 68
Psalms 135:4 36
Psalms 145:18 104
Psalms 145:18 30
Psalms 146:3 59
Proverbs 1:8 122
Proverbs 7:4-5 123
Proverbs 21:1 70
Proverbs 21:13 46
Proverbs 21:16 32
Ecclesiastes 1:1-2 133
Lamentations 2:13 127
Lamentations 2:13 24
Lamentations 3:1-4 25

Lamentations 22:6 149
Isaiah 5:8 178
Isaiah 6:8-10 151
Isaiah 25:28. 10
Isaiah 40:18 90
Isaiah 51:12 88
Jeremiah 7:3 130
Jeremiah 30:22 132
Jeremiah 31:14 78
Hosea 1:2 15
Hosea 8:5 13
Jonah 2:1-3 34
Habakuk 1:12 35
Zechariah 1:7-10 56
Malachi 4:5-6 60
Esther 8:16 138
I Maccabees 2:27 203

New Testament
Matthew 1:1 72
Matthew 1:17 23
Matthew 5 173
Matthew 6:26 89
Matthew 2:19-21.23 86
Mark 5:1-2, 11-13 97
Mark16:6-8 108
Luke 3:23, 31 120
Luke 24:50-51 161

John 1:45-46 131
John 14:5-6 181
John 21:25 196
Acts 28:28 199
Hebrews 12:1-4). 204
1 Timothy 2:13-14 201

Other Writings
Amidah 57
Amidah 153
Avot de Rabi Natan 30 177
Baraita of R. Ishmael 125
Haggadah, liturgy for the Pass-
over Seder 120
Mishnah Avot 1:6 152
Mishnah Avot 1:7 38
Mishnah Avot 4:1. 9
Nefilat Apayim 27
Nefilat Apayim 49
Pesuqei de-Zimra 81
Quran Al-Karim, Sura 107:1-3
83
Rashi's commentary on Num-
bers 12:13 100
Saint Wolfgang 146
Talmud Berakhot 60b 69
Talmud Gitin 6b 87
Talmud Taanit 29a 16
Zionist saying 20